WORK, AGING, AND VISION

Report of a Conference

Working Group on Aging Workers and Visual Impairment

Committee on Vision

Commission on Behavioral and Social Sciences
and Education

National Research Council

National Academy Press
Washington, D.C. 1987

NOTICE: The project that is the subject of this report was approved by the Governing Board of the National Research Council, whose members are drawn from the councils of the National Academy of Sciences, the National Academy of Engineering, and the Institute of Medicine. The members of the committee responsible for the report were chosen for their special competences and with regard for appropriate balance.

This report has been reviewed by a group other than the authors according to procedures approved by a Report Review Committee consisting of members of the National Academy of Sciences, the National Academy of Engineering, and the Institute of Medicine.

The National Research Council was established by the National Academy of Sciences in 1916 to associate the broad community of science and technology with the Academy's purposes of furthering knowledge and of advising the federal government. The Council operates in accordance with general policies determined by the Academy under the authority of its congressional charter of 1863, which establishes the Academy as a private nonprofit, self-governing membership corporation. The Council has become the principal operating agency of both the National Academy of Sciences and the National Academy of Engineering in the conduct of their services to the government, the public, and the scientific and engineering communities. It is administered jointly by both Academies and the Institute of Medicine. The National Academy of Engineering and the Institute of Medicine were established in 1964 and 1970, respectively, under the charter of the National Academy of Sciences.

This work relates to Department of the Navy contract N0014-80-C-0159 issued by the Office of Naval Research under Contract Authority NR 201-124. However, the content does not necessarily reflect the position or the policy of the government, and no official endorsement should be inferred.

The United States government has at least a royalty-free, nonexclusive, and irrevocable license throughout the world for government purposes to publish, translate, reproduce, deliver, perform, dispose of, and to authorize others to do, all or any portion of this work.

Available from:
Committee on Vision
National Research Council
2101 Constitution Avenue N.W.
Washington, D.C. 20418

Printed in the United States of America

WORKING GROUP ON AGING WORKERS AND VISUAL IMPAIRMENT

ROBERT SEKULER (Chair), Departments of Psychology, Ophthalmology, and Neurobiology/Physiology, Northwestern University

STEVEN FERRIS, School of Medicine, New York University

SAMUEL M. GENENSKY, The Center for the Partially Sighted, Santa Monica, Calif.

ROBERT GOTTSDANKER, Department of Psychology, University of California, Santa Barbara

DONALD KLINE, Department of Psychology, University of Notre Dame

DAVID D. MICHAELS, Department of Ophthalmology, University of California, Los Angeles

MEREDITH MORGAN, Walnut Creek, Calif.

DONALD G. PITTS, College of Optometry, University of Houston

COMMITTEE ON VISION

ANTHONY J. ADAMS (Chair), School of Optometry, University of California, Berkeley
ROBERT SEKULER (Past Chair), Departments of Psychology, Ophthalmology, and Neurobiology/Physiology, Northwestern University
IRVING BIEDERMAN, Department of Psychology, State University of New York, Buffalo
RANDOLPH BLAKE, Cresap Neuroscience Laboratory, Northwestern University
RONALD E. CARR, New York University Medical Center
SHELDON EBENHOLTZ, State University of New York, College of Optometry
ANN B. FULTON, Department of Ophthalomology, Children's Hospital, Boston
CHRIS A. JOHNSON, Department of Ophthalmology, University of California, Davis
JO ANN KINNEY, vision consultant, Surry, Maine
AZRIEL ROSENFELD, Center for Automation Research, University of Maryland

PAMELA EBERT FLATTAU, Study Director
CAROL METCALF, Senior Secretary

Foreword

The Committee on Vision is a standing committee of the National Research Council's Commission on Behavioral and Social Sciences and Education. The committee provides analysis and advice on scientific issues and applied problems involving vision. It also attempts to stimulate the further development of visual science and to provide a forum in which basic and applied scientists, engineers, and clinicians can interact. Working groups of the committee study questions that may involve engineering and equipment, physiological and physical optics, neurophysiology, psychophysics, perception, environmental effects on vision, and the treatment of visual disorders.

In order for the committee to perform its role effectively, it draws on experts from a wide range of scientific, engineering, and clinical disciplines. The members of this working group were chosen for their expertise in research related to the aging of the human eye and for their familiarity with the application of those research findings to employment issues. This report reflects their evaluation of present understanding of the interactive effects of work, aging, and vision. The report outlines the nature of the problem and describes some of the solutions that have emerged as employers have attempted to sustain the employment of older persons given the changes that occur in vision with age. The report considers the scientific, technological, and social contexts for enhancing the employment of older workers and provides an agenda for further research in this area.

The observations and recommendations arising from the efforts of this working group merit consideration by employers and employees alike, and by those clinicians and scientists interested in improving the employment and employability of older workers.

Anthony J. Adams, Chair
Committee on Vision

Contents

PREFACE ix

1 NATURE OF THE PROBLEM 1
   Vision Changes and Older Workers, 4
   Vision Screening Programs in the Workplace, 17
   Matching Workers and Jobs, 20
   Workplace Design, 22
   Responding to the Vision Needs of Older Workers, 24

2 SOLUTIONS 28
   Compensating for Declining Visual Function, 28
   Better Vision Screening Procedures, 31
   Providing Visual Aids, 32
   Retraining Older Workers, 33
   Modifying the Workplace, 35
   Job Redesign, 37

3 CONTEXT FOR CHANGE 38
   The Potential of Science and Technology, 39
   Employer Commitment as a Critical Element
      for Change, 44
   Federal Programs and Policies, 45
   Conclusion, 47

APPENDIX A: Conference Participants and Program 49

APPENDIX B: Annotated Bibliography 54

Preface

At the request of the Veterans Administration and the National Institute on Aging, the Committee on Vision established the Working Group on Aging Workers and Visual Impairment. The working group was asked to examine the issue of keeping older workers in the work force longer given the many changes that occur in vision with age.

In order to accomplish its task, the working group organized an invitational conference to review the dimensions of the problem of work, aging, and vision. Twenty-eight specialists, including members of the working group, met for two days in Washington, D.C., in February 1986 (see Appendix A for the conference participants and program.) These specialists were drawn from the fields of gerontology, economics, sociology, statistics, psychology, political science, optometry, ophthalmology, human factors engineering, and physiology.

The two-day conference was organized around sessions focusing on individual and interactive elements of work, aging, and vision. Members of the first panel were asked to describe what happens to the eye with age; some relationships between visual changes with age and changes in behavior; and the impact of visual deficits on cognitive functions. The second panel considered the availability of information on the incidence and prevalence of visual impairment with age; the role of health status in leaving the work force; and demographic changes in the U.S. work force. The third panel explored the effects of visual changes on job skills; problems of performance assessment; and relevant components of "bona fide occupational qualifications." The fourth panel addressed issues related to keeping older Americans in the work force longer, such as screening practices; the availability of visual prosthetics; job and task redesign; work station design; and economic incentives and disincentives for keeping older workers employed.

Each participant prepared a brief background paper, which was circulated in advance of the meeting. Participants were asked to provide a brief presentation of their papers at the conference. Scheduled discussion periods allowed extensive treatment of the panel topics and included questions and comments from the audience.

This report is based on those conference papers and discussions and has been organized into three parts. The first part is a discussion of the problem of maintaining older workers in the labor force given the changes that occur in vision with age. The report then shifts to a description of some of the solutions proposed by conferees. The final section explores some of the factors involved in bringing about such changes.

Two appendixes provide additional information: Appendix A contains a list of conference participants and the detailed program. Appendix B contains an annotated bibliography on work, aging, and vision.

In addition to the 28 participants at the conference, a number of people contributed in important ways to the success of the conference and to this report. Samuel M. Genensky and Herbert Parnes prepared background papers for the conference, although they were unable to attend. David Worthen of the Veterans Administration and Leonard Jakubczak of the National Institute on Aging provided valuable guidance as project monitors to the working group throughout this effort. Wayne Shebilske, the committee's study director through June 1985, planned the working group activity, and Pamela Ebert Flattau, the committee's study director after July 1985, provided important assistance in organizing the conference and preparing the workshop report. Patricia A. Anderson, who served as consultant to the committee on this project, contributed significantly to the design and scope of the February conference. Christine L. McShane, editor of the Commission on

Behavioral and Social Sciences and Education, helped improve the style and clarity of the report. Carol Metcalf, the committee's senior secretary, provided valuable secretarial and administrative assistance. To all of these people, we express our gratitude for their efforts.

Robert Sekuler, Chair
Working Group on Aging Workers
and Visual Impairment

1
Nature of the Problem

The aging of the human eye involves a series of changes in visual performance that can be detected readily in the healthy adult. After age 40, visual acuity, range of focus, and color discrimination decrease and sensitivity to glare increases. These changes can lead cumulatively to significant visual deterioration in older people.

Viewed in the context of employment, reduced visual function does not necessarily have any effect on job performance—but for some individuals, it will. This may be due to the fact that their work environment is not appropriately designed for visually demanding tasks, because they have other health problems that exacerbate the effects of declining visual function, or because their vision problems remain uncorrected. The negative consequences of age-related vision changes may include lower productivity, increased frequency of accidents, greater absenteeism, and ultimately the decision to leave the work force.

It is of course in an employer's interest to be sensitive to the vision needs of older workers—indeed, of all workers. A firm may save considerable time and money in building and sustaining a productive work force through health care and employment policies that give vision a prominent role. And since an increasing proportion of the population will be over 40 in coming years, the growing number of older workers may require the development of strategies to make their labor force participation more productive.

Many firms already sponsor vision screening programs, typically as part of preplacement and periodic physical examinations. Screening procedures are often limited to visual acuity testing, although other facets of vision may be tested given the physical requirements of a job and safety considerations. For jobs in some companies, for example, color vision may be tested because normal color vision is important for sorting complicated, color-coded electrical wiring. For jobs in other companies, in which depth perception is crucial for the safe handling of dangerous material, stereopsis—one aspect of depth perception—may be monitored so that workers will not present a danger to themselves or their coworkers.

Screening tests are used to determine whether an individual's vision is adequate for a certain job, or whether certain restrictions should be placed by the employer on a worker's performance of a job. For example, if a worker has experienced the loss of certain parts of the visual field through disease, the employer may wish to reassign the worker to a task that involves less detailed work. Alternatively, the employer may simply decide to keep the worker at the job but change the lighting conditions surrounding the task. For vision screening procedures to be effective for these various purposes, it is vital that the screening tests match the requirements of the task.

On average, the visual functions of older workers differ significantly from those of younger workers. These visual functions can and should be identified and tested. Many of the vision screening tests used today are inadequate to test the full visual capabilities of older workers. The tests frequently have no relevance to the work to be performed—a problem that affects all workers. The screening procedures, furthermore, are not likely to include tests designed to detect the visual changes of older workers—changes that could impair job performance. And perhaps what is worse, older workers may be employed in job settings in which no thought has been given to vision screening or to their vision needs.

About 25 million Americans are 65 and older; that figure will double in the next 25 years. And in the next 15 years, the baby boom will continue to increase the number of middle-aged workers. The demographic changes occurring in the U.S. labor force suggest that many employers should become more interested in the role of vision screening, job placement, and environmental design for sustaining the productivity and employability of workers. Several things are necessary, though, before employers who are interested in doing so will have the means to introduce or improve programs that take into account age-related changes in vision. First, more information is needed from scientists on the implications of age-related changes in vision for the performance of specific tasks—whether in manufacturing industries, information services, or other employment sectors. While vision research has generated a great deal of information about age-related visual changes in contrast sensitivity, color vision, and acuity, the connection between those vision changes and job performance needs to be more clearly demonstrated. Furthermore, much of this knowledge about vision changes with age is based on studies of individuals under the age of 65.

Second, more information is needed about the vision screening programs already in place in businesses throughout the nation. It is important to establish whether the vision tests currently being administered are appropriate for detecting the visual changes that normally occur with age and whether they are job relevant. It is also important to determine if other vision tests are available or could be developed for use with older workers. Third, more information is needed about job placement programs based on the visual capabilities of workers. Some companies have introduced job coding systems that include specification of vision skills. We need to assess the extent to which this approach has application for older workers and in settings other than the ones in which job coding is currently being used.

Finally, it is important to develop and disseminate information on how work stations and the work environment could be made more responsive to the vision needs of older workers. Although there is much information currently available on environmental design, only a portion of it addresses the vision needs of older workers. Much more could be done in this area. It should be made clear at the outset that the terms *older worker* or *aging worker* do not correspond to a particular worker or a particular age group. Visual processes age at different rates and present problems for people at different stages of their lives. Loss of focusing power (presbyopia), for example, typically manifests itself in people in their forties, but the ability to resolve moving targets (dynamic acuity) may not deteriorate for most people until they are well into their seventies. Moreover, for any single visual function, such as dynamic acuity, there are substantial differences among individuals of the same chronological age. We should also make clear that there is no "typical" older worker. There are huge differences between individuals with respect to any one of the vision problems that are the subject of this report.

VISION CHANGES AND OLDER WORKERS

Although there is a sizable literature on aging and vision, little of this research has addressed the special problems of vision in the work setting. A useful first step would be the identification of those changes in vision with age relevant to an individual's ability to work, some of which are detailed below.

Smaller Pupil Size and Loss of Focusing Ability

While there are many normal changes of significance in the nondiseased aging eye, the most functionally important changes seem to be the reduction in pupil size and the loss of accommodative or focusing ability. The area of the pupil governs the amount of light that can reach the retina. Because of smaller pupil size, older eyes receive much less light at the retina. At the conference, Ian Bailey reported that the light-adapted eye of a 20-year-old receives six times more light than that of an 80-year-old. In dark-adapted conditions, the 20-year-old eye receives about 16 times more light. In comparison to younger persons, it is as though older persons were wearing medium-density sunglasses in bright light and extremely dark glasses in very dim light. Thus, for any detailed visually guided tasks on which performance varies with illumination, older workers require extra lighting.

Presbyopia is the most common visual disorder in later life. This lack of accommodative ability limits the range of usable working distances. Substituting an inflexible spectacle lens for a flexible ciliary lens places the older person at a distinct disadvantage. The range of clear vision is restricted, particularly for intermediate distances. Many machines and tasks (computers, music stands, library shelves, etc.) are not designed for comfortable bifocal viewing, requiring fatiguing and inefficient postural contortions. Nor do trifocals and variable focal lenses always solve the problem if they restrict the visual field and create new aberrations or awkward head and eye positions. When the task involves moving, climbing, or otherwise navigating under conditions of precarious stability, the presbyope may be a hazard to himself or herself as well as to others.

Color vision and contrast sensitivity are also known to be affected by aging. Color vision changes cause some reduction of the ability to discriminate blues and blue-greens. The normal yellowing of the lens of the eye is believed to be chiefly responsible for this effect.

The aging lens and cornea often cause glare by light scattering, especially for shorter wavelengths. Stray light and lenticular fluorescence washes out contrast. It is possible, however, that the reduction in retinal luminance due to smaller pupil size also contributes to contrast sensitivity loss in older persons.

In summary, reduced pupil size and loss of focusing ability are two changes in vision that naturally occur with age. These changes, along with lens yellowing and light scattering by the ocular media, are probably the most significant changes in the older eye having some effect on an individual's ability to work. Disease cannot be ignored, however, as a contributing factor to ocular changes and is addressed in the next section.

Disease-Related Visual Disabilities

Disease is the most common cause of visual disability. Not only do systemic illnesses such as arteriosclerosis, hypertension, and diabetes have ocular consequences, but also the drugs used to control them can have visual side effects. Topical ocular diseases are also more prevalent with aging. For example, the Framingham eye study showed that acuity losses in the elderly could be accounted for by four major diseases: cataract, macular degeneration, other retinal pathology, and glaucoma.[1] Ninety percent of persons age 65 and older whose better eye had a visual acuity of 20/30 or worse also had one of the four diseases. Such data clearly suggest where the emphasis (and cost-effectiveness) of prevention and treatment should be placed.

David Michaels observed at the conference that not only are the elderly prone to certain diseases, but they are also prone to the aggregate effects of illnesses whose onset is earlier and that may even be congenital. This pathological background must always be considered in the diagnosis of vision problems.

Some eye diseases have major functional consequences resulting from a loss of visual field or contrast sensitivity. Objects, obstacles, and hazards in the periphery become undetectable and

---

[1] Leibowitz, H.M., D.E. Krueger, L.R. Maunder, R.C. Milton, M.M. Kini, H.A. Kahn, R.J. Nickerson, J. Pool, T.L. Colton, J.P. Ganley, J.I. Loewenstein, and T.R. Dawber (1980), *The Framingham Eye Study Monograph Survey of Ophthalmology*. Vol. 24 (Supplement) May-June.

mobility (either ambulatory or vehicular) becomes unsafe, particularly in congested and complex environments. Indeed, Chris Johnson told conferees that when visual field loss is extensive, it can create a significant visual disability, especially for tasks involving spatial orientation or mobility skills.

Johnson and his colleagues examined driving accident and conviction records of 10,000 persons for a 3-year period prior to testing to determine the relationship between peripheral visual function and driving performance.[2] Persons with visual field abnormalities were divided into two groups: (1) visual field loss in only one eye and (2) visual field loss in both eyes. The driving records of age and sex-matched control subjects with normal visual fields were obtained for comparison. No differences were found in the accident and conviction rates of individuals with visual field loss in only one eye and their control group. However, the group with visual field loss in both eyes had more than twice as many accidents and convictions as their control group with normal visual fields. Johnson has concluded that binocular visual field loss is associated with poorer driving performance.

Most visual disorders mentioned in this section produce a reduction of contrast sensitivity, but, as Bailey told conferees, glaucoma and cataracts produce the most marked reductions. With these two conditions, visual acuity can remain good while contrast sensitivity can be functionally impaired. This has substantial implications for tasks involving mobility. An example of a task requiring good contrast sensitivity is the recognition of steps or stairs. Often the treads and risers of stairs are made of the same material, so that it is only relative shading created by the lighting that allows the viewer to distinguish the horizontal faces from the vertical faces of the steps. The differences in brightness are often rather small. Bailey concluded that using steps or stairs is a significant challenge to individuals with reduced contrast sensitivity, given that the task of identifying steps is one of detecting contrast differences rather than one of resolving spatial detail.

In addition to the effects of normal aging of the eye, then, the functional consequences of disease must be considered in any discussion of ocular changes among older workers. Restricted visual

---

[2] Johnson, C.A., and J.L. Keltner (1983), The incidence of visual field loss in 20,000 eyes and its relationship to driving performance. *Archives of Ophthalmology* 101:371-376.

fields, reduced contrast sensitivity, and diminished color vision are perhaps the most significant disease-related visual changes that influence an individual's ability to function in the work setting.

Effects of Reduced Visual Functioning on Job Performance

It is one thing to say that an older worker may have reduced contrast sensitivity, and another to trace the implications of such impairment to a particular job. Interviews with older workers, laboratory research, task analysis, and statistical analysis were among the techniques suggested at the conference to achieve that goal.

For example, Meredith Morgan evaluated the decline in his own visual performance in a variety of tasks for purposes of the conference. Morgan told conferees:

> The most aggravating aspect of my vision today is the feeling that it doesn't work as effortlessly or as quickly as it did when I was younger. It seems to me that I must concentrate harder now and that I require higher levels of illumination than I formerly did in order to have the same perceptual results. Just plain seeing in simplified situations, as in routine vision testing, seems as good and as quick as ever—but perceiving the meaning of a complex, changing scene is definitely more difficult and slower. I see the parts almost as well as I ever did but the organizing of the perception as a whole seems to be more time-consuming and to require more attention.

Self-reports by older persons about their visual problems can be of tremendous help in understanding the consequences of visual aging in work settings. Clinicians have long recognized the importance of self-reporting. Michaels repeated an old maxim: "To define an illness, don't ask the doctor—ask the patient." Scientific investigators may make significant advances in understanding the consequences of age-related changes in vision on job performance simply by asking older workers what problems they have noticed. Examples of that approach are described in the next section.

Surveys of Visual Problems of Older People

William Kosnik reported to conferees that he and his colleagues at Northwestern University have developed a survey technique that requires people to rate their own visual disabilities. This survey technique provides valuable insights into the changing visual capabilities of older persons in much the same way as reports by older workers themselves. Respondents, ranging in age from 18 to 95, were asked to rate how often they encountered difficulty with their vision in each situation described. The first problem area to emerge from the survey was slower speed in visual processing. This relates to the time it takes to perform a variety of visual tasks. Respondents reported that it took them more time to read than it did when they were younger. They were also less confident in performing tasks that depended on vision, such as going down steps, driving, doing hobbies, and the like.

A second problem area involved difficulty seeing under conditions of poor illumination. Respondents reported having difficulty in distinguishing dark colors, such as distinguishing dark blue socks from black socks.

Another problem area had to do with adapting to bright lights. Respondents reported having problems adjusting to bright lighting when going from a movie theater into daylight, for example.

In order to determine how these visual problem areas change with age, Kosnik divided the sample into an older group and a younger group, using a cutoff at the age of 50. The analysis showed that the older group had greater difficulty in the first two areas. These results indicate that the processing of visual input slows with age and that older people are adversely affected when lighting conditions are less than ideal. The third age-related visual problem area, adapting to bright lights, was a complaint more commonly expressed by the younger group.

In summary, the survey work described by Kosnik identified several visual problem areas for older adults. The fact that older adults themselves recognize these limitations suggests that they are serious enough to have impact on the way they perform their daily activities. Of course, survey research does not specify how much illumination should be increased or how much more slowly visual tasks would need to be presented in order for older workers to perform the task safely and comfortably. Empirical research is providing the answers to some of these questions. A survey approach can, however, help to identify some of the everyday vision challenges that are likely to trouble older adults.

Laboratory Research

Laboratory research has improved understanding of a number of problems of visual perception that tend to accompany aging and may have relevance to job performance. One example of a problem that has benefited from laboratory research is the decreased ability to deal with visual clutter. Robert Sekuler described for conferees a laboratory analogue to a visual problem that seems to be fairly common among older people: difficulty picking out one target from a cluster of targets. The research rests on the observation that, despite good acuity and fairly normal visual fields, an older person may experience difficulty spotting a friend in a crowd or reading a street sign in the midst of other signs. The task in Sekuler's laboratory analogue was to report where on a television screen a cartoon face had been briefly presented—a task sometimes called "radial localization."

The target cartoon face was presented randomly on various meridia and at any one of three different eccentricities from fixation. The target was followed by a spatially random mask that effectively limited visual processing to the period during which the face was actually on the television screen. Both older and younger observers performed equally well and virtually without error. One would conclude from these results that the two groups were equivalent in radial localization ability.

However, when the target cartoon face was presented in the midst of "distractor" targets (small rectangles), the older observers' performance declined precipitously; the younger observers' performance was affected only slightly. Sekuler concluded that, under conditions that mimic those of everyday life, the functional visual fields of older observers appear to be dramatically constricted.

The simulation method is another experimental technique designed to increase understanding of visual problems among older persons. One example of simulation studies may be found in the work of Leon Pastalan.[3] Pastalan's empathic model is a technique that simulates selected age-related visual changes while an observer engages in various everyday tasks.

Specially designed lenses worn by young observers simulate a combination of reduced retinal illumination and degraded retinal image. These lenses have a coating that both diffuses and attenuates (by 25 percent) the passing light. The lenses reduce the acuity of the wearer, although the reduction is thought to underrepresent the extent of deterioration actually experienced by many older people.

Participants in Pastalan's simulation studies have reported that glare from uncontrolled natural light and from unbalanced artificial light sources was the single most ubiquitous difficulty encountered. For instance, when participants walked up an aisle toward the front of a supermarket, the typical vast expanse of plate glass across the front of the store obliterated most of the detail surrounding objects on bright days. Single intense artificial light sources produced more uncomfortable glare than combinations of less intense sources. Participants reported a number of other problems:

1. Glare from uncontrolled natural light and from unbalanced artificial light sources.
2. Color fading (green/blue, most; red, least).
3. Difficulty perceiving the boundary between two contrasting surfaces, especially when two intense colors bounded each other.
4. Difficulty perceiving boundary between two related colors.
5. Depth perception was affected.
6. Adjusting to changes in illumination when moving from lighted area to dark area or vice versa.
7. Impairment of ability to discriminate fine detail.

There are limits to what laboratory research and simulation techniques can tell us about the vision problems of older workers. For example, one aspect of perception that has been extensively researched in the laboratory from the perspective of aging concerns the speed or rapidity of perception. Speed of perception

---

[3] Pastalan, L.A. (1982), Environmental design and adaptation to the visual environment. In R. Sekuler, D. Kline, and K. Dismukes, eds., *Aging and Human Visual Function*. New York: Alan R. Liss, Inc.

has been investigated with a number of laboratory procedures; the universal finding in research of this type is that adults with average ages in the sixties and seventies are either less accurate or require significantly longer durations to achieve the same degree of accuracy than adults with an average age of about 20.

Because the rapidity, selectivity, and integration of perception are likely to be important elements in many complex occupational tasks, one might expect to find pronounced age-related impairments in a great many job activities dependent on quick perceptual processing. In fact, however, there have been remarkably few well-documented, age-associated decrements in job performance. Notable exceptions are in the areas of professional athletics and certain jobs with severe time stresses. For the most part, one is struck by how few age effects have been found in actual work performance in which quick perceptual processing is involved.

Timothy Salthouse suggested to conferees that there might be several possible reasons for this failure to find age differences in work effectiveness comparable to those observed in laboratory studies. Laboratory assessments may be more demanding than the evaluations typically performed concerning job effectiveness. It is also possible that adults, particularly older adults, are more motivated to perform well in their work activities than in the rather abstract tasks encountered in most research laboratories. A third interpretation of this discrepancy between laboratory and the workplace relates to the amount of experience people have had on the tasks in which performance is being evaluated. Because many laboratory tasks are deliberately designed to minimize the influences of experience outside the laboratory, they can be considered to consist of comparisons of novices. However, because most people have spent thousands of hours performing the activities of their job or daily life, they can be considered to be experts in these activities. Thus, results from the laboratory may not be generalizable to real-world situations.

David Walsh concurred with the view that the lab-life connection needs to be strengthened. He suggested that more knowledge is needed about the validity of basic information processing measures as predictors of everyday seeing. Knowing what to assess will also depend on the importance of particular stages of perceptual processing to a specific job. Finally, Walsh suggested, we need to know more about the underlying causes of perceptual changes.

Walsh added, as did a number of other conferees, that another important problem is that of individual differences. Not every older person shows the same decrement in a perceptual task, and a few older people actually perform a task better than some younger people. The primary implication is that investigators must take into account in designing their experiment that chronological age is not a very strong predictor of an individual's visual performance.

In summary, laboratory research, surveys, and simulation methods can contribute to understanding of the vision problems encountered by older workers as they age. Scientists will, however, have to address two significant methodological issues if the findings from such research are to have practical application. The first challenge is to develop better matches between visually oriented laboratory tools and the real-world tasks being studied. The other challenge is to arrive at abetter understanding of the factors that account for the high degree of individual differences reported by many investigators.

On-Site, On-the-Job Research

Although some data are available regarding visual ability and driving performance, for other jobs that are predominantly visual in nature—such as visual inspection tasks or work at video display terminals—the data are limited on how performance is affected by changes that occur in vision with age. Pauline K. Robinson told conferees that the issue concerns the value of keeping older workers in the work force longer. Employers may find that the most convincing evidence for changing their employment practices comes from on-site, on-the-job research that measures visual decline and task performance.

Although data are limited regarding how changes in visual function affect the performance of specific tasks, conference participants reported on one or two studies that have advanced understanding of this topic through field research. James Fozard described a study carried out by the National Institute on Aging's Gerontology Research Center that sought to minimize age differences in performance through optimal office lighting. The investigators found that by increasing the illumination level in the office, the performance of clerical workers improved, with greater improvement evident among the older workers. Both groups expressed a preference for higher levels of illumination, but only the older group reported greater eye comfort at the highest light level used in the study. This type of field research, according to Fozard, could significantly increase understanding of the specific vision needs of older workers.

The Illuminating Engineering Society of North America (IES) has conducted on-site task analyses to guide the development of lighting recommendations in a variety of settings, including the work setting. Such analyses may provide a useful starting point for researchers interested in on-the-job studies of vision among older workers.

Alan Lewis, who is chair of the committee on lighting standards of IES, explained to conferees that when illumination levels are established by the IES for a specific location, the recommendations are developed through a multistage process. For interior spaces, such as offices, the procedure starts with the identification and classification of the visual task into "task categories" that have broad illuminance requirements based on task contrast, size, and duration. At this stage, the illuminance recommendations consist of a range of values; the selection of a value within the range is based on weighting factors that depend on: (1) the average age of the worker in the space, (2) the demand for speed and/or accuracy, and (3) the task background reflectance. For the age factor, a certain number is assigned to ages under 40, another assigned to ages 40-55, and yet another is assigned to ages over 55. This factor is included to acknowledge the fact that older persons suffer from increased disability glare and have reduced contrast sensitivity.

As an example, a typewritten page calls for an illuminance of from 200 lux to 500 lux. If the worker's age was 60 and the demand for accuracy was important, the illuminance recommendation would be 300 lux. The recommendation for a worker age 30 performing the same task would be 200 lux.

Thousands of tasks have thus been analyzed by the IES, although Lewis added that the illuminance selection is only a starting point in the lighting design process. Freedom from direct glare and veiling reflections, color considerations, and myriad other factors are every bit as important to the effectiveness of the lighted space as is illumination level. A lesser amount of good quality illuminance can often be far more visually effective than a larger amount of light from a poorly designed lighting system. Guidance on potential problems and recommended solutions for particular types of spaces can be found in the IES publications.[4]

One of the greatest challenges to investigators interested in the effects of age changes in vision on job performance is the role of prior experience in visually guided tasks. Sara Czaja told conferees that, if we look at an inspection task and break it down into task components—visual search (in which one searches an item, a target, or a flaw) and decision making (in which one sees something and decides whether it falls within acceptable standards), a nonintuitive result occurs. One would expect age decrements on those kinds of tasks based on the reports in the literature. However, the data are limited and far from conclusive. One study found a slight age-related decline in the ability to discriminate between flawed and unflawed items; another reported no age effects; and a third showed a decrease in inspection error with age. According to Czaja, recent studies suggest that the amount of decrement in visual search tasks may depend on familiarity with the task. In other words, well-practiced visual search activities may not exhibit age-related decline. Clearly, cognitive factors such as skill level need to be taken into account in any study of the impact of visual changes on task performance, as Salthouse also demonstrated.

Statistical Reporting Systems

As Stephen McConnell told conferees, there is a perception among lawmakers and the general public that because people are living longer, they are healthier. We really don't know if this assumption is correct or what people mean by the term *healthy*.

Several studies indicate that workers are retiring from the labor force at much younger ages than previously. They may chose to do so to enjoy the benefits of good health in their retirement years or they may decide to retire because of health problems. Declining vision could well be among those reasons why older workers leave the labor force, whether voluntarily or involuntarily.

In a paper prepared for the conference, Herbert Parnes reported that the average retirement age is now about 62, and for large corporations it is closer to 59. Why do workers retire? In

---

[4] Kaufman, John E. ed. (1984), *IES Lighting Handbook: Reference*. New York: Illuminating Engineering Society of North America; (1987), *IES Lighting Handbook: Application*. New York: Illuminating Engineering Society of North America.

recent years the mandatory retirement age in many occupations has been increased from age 65 to 70. Parnes, using evidence from longitudinal surveys, found that, of almost 8 million retired men between the ages of 60 and 74, only 3 percent were required to retire.

As many as 56 percent of the retirees appear to have freely chosen retirement, and 35 percent had retired for reasons of health. While Parnes acknowledges that there is a conceptual problem in distinguishing between retirement for reasons of health and voluntary retirement, his longitudinal evidence indicates that the categorization is sound. Some of the retirements for reasons of health have to do with defective vision, but it is difficult to find the data that indicate the extent.

Certain federal statistical reporting systems may have a role in understanding how declining vision influences job decisions among older workers. Richard Burkhauser described the results of a pseudoclinical study that one of his students conducted using data from the Social Security Administration.[5] Mitchell was interested in the effects of the early onset of arthritis in work force participation. She found that individuals who developed arthritis at age 40 stayed in the work force 12 more years on average. The comparison group, who reported no health impairments at age 40, stayed in the work force 23 more years. Burkhauser suggested that similar studies might be conducted to determine the effects of the early onset of visual impairments on work force participation by age.

The data from a number of surveys carry information about prevalence of visual impairment, disability, and employment handicap and were described for conferees by Corinne Kirchner. As she pointed out, however, there are many problems with these data of which investigators should be aware. The terms *pathology, impairment, disability*, and *handicap* mean different things in different surveys. Most surveys have neglected the older population because that group has not been considered of importance; the samples are not always sufficiently large or representative of the older population. Still, the data bases (Table 1) could be of considerable interest to investigators.

---

[5] Mitchell, Jean M. (1986), The Effect of Arthritis in Work Behavior. Unpublished doctoral dissertation, Vanderbilt University, May.

TABLE 1 Characteristics of Data Bases Related to Prevalence of Visual Impairment, Disability, and Employment Handicap

Agency/Name of Data Base	Date(s)	Concept/Measure of Visual Problem	Method of Data Collection	Population Covered	Employment Status Measures
National Center for Health Statistics					
a. Health Examination Survey	1960-62 1971-72	Specific visual impairments, e.g. acuity, motility	Standardized examinations	National non-institutional samples	Minimal
b. Health Interview Survey	annual (some items at longer intervals)	Pre-1982: reading disability; selected impairments and pathologies; handicap Post-1982: dropped reading disability	Standardized interview, self or proxy reports	" "	Minimal
Bureau of the Census					
a. Survey of Income and Education	1976	"Serious difficulty seeing or blind" (disability), asked if limited in major roles (handicap)	" "	" "	Considerable
b. Decennial census	1990	Planned measure not yet specified	Self-administered questionnaire	Total population or large sample	Minimal
Social Security Administration "Work and Disability" Surveys	1966 1972 1978	Impairment, disability (gross and detailed visual tasks), handicap	Standardized interviews	National non-institutional samples - (16, 18, or 20) through 64 years	Comprehensive
National Society to Prevent Blindness	1978, projected from 1970	Impairment (acuity of 20/200 or less, better eye, best correction or field of 20° or less)	Estimating formula applied to data from selected state registers of legal blindness	Total population who are legally blind (but see method of data collection)	None

Ronald Wilson told conferees that the 1990 census may carry questions about conditions (including vision) that limit working, driving, and the like. These questions are being pretested at the present time and, if included in the 1990 census, could be another source of information for studies in this area.

VISION SCREENING PROGRAMS IN THE WORKPLACE

Data are inadequate on many problems that relate to visual impairment, aging, and the workplace. But no lack is more keenly felt than the near-total ignorance about the policies of large American companies in this area. Of particular importance are company policies on vision screening. For example, what do large companies do to screen their workers' vision? What steps are taken for periodic vision testing? What procedures are available for adjusting the workers' job environment in order to accommodate visual problems?

Some answers to these questions were provided by two conference participants representing companies with active vision care programs. Roberta Alex of Convair Division, General Dynamics Corporation, a defense contractor, described the screening program at that company. Alex explained that preplacement screening examinations are performed to match the physical capabilities of an applicant with available jobs. Such a match considers job-related physical requirements, the work environment, and the safe performance of the job. The physical examination includes a complete history and physical examination—including visual acuity. The medical services office also routinely performs several thousand visual acuity certification tests on employees each year. If presbyopia develops, employees are required to obtain prescription lenses to meet job requirements. Alex added that employees may take advantage of the eye care program that provides a complete examination, lenses, and frames at a discount.

Louise Birkholz of the Chicago-based S&C Electric Company described that company's program. The company has been in business since 1911 and manufactures high-voltage switches and fuses used by electric utilities and other large power consumers. S&C's company-sponsored vision-protection program dates back over 30 years. In the early 1950s, this company made the decision to provide all employees with "appropriate" safety glasses (prescription glasses, if necessary). An optometrist came to the plant and gave eye examinations to all employees. To make the eye examination process as easy as possible, appointments were scheduled during working hours, minimizing excuses not to keep appointments. Plano and prescription safety glasses were then purchased by the company for employees in need of them.

Following that initial round of examinations in the 1950s, the optometrist currently visits the company once or twice a month for follow-up examinations and examinations of new employees. An ophthalmologist is on call in case of eye injury or if special eye problems are detected by the optometrist.

Employees receiving S&C-sponsored eye examinations include all new employees in manufacturing areas. For all employees age 60 and over, the company sponsors annual physical examinations in addition to the annual eye examination. Employees who are vehicle operators, such as forklift drivers, and all employees who work in the solid-state assembly area are examined annually. Employees in manufacturing areas are examined once every two years, or sooner if necessary.

The management of both S&C Electric and Convair consider their vision programs cost-effective. The companies believe that the expense of running the vision programs is offset by improved productivity, retention of highly experienced workers, and job satisfaction.

There are ways for workers with vision problems to receive care other than through their place of employment. If they are veterans, they may turn to the Veterans Administration (VA). Joseph Maino described one such program. VICTORS (Vision Impairment Center to Optimize Remaining Sight) is a low-vision rehabilitation program designed to optimize services to the partially sighted and complement existing eye clinics and blind rehabilitation centers.

VICTORS' main goal is to keep working veterans on the job and return unemployed veterans to the work force. The VICTORS staff: (1) assists the visually impaired veteran to optimize remaining vision, (2) suggests ways to modify work conditions or job task to better suit veterans' abilities, (3) refers eligible veterans for vocational rehabilitation training, or (4) refers veterans to state vocational rehabilitation agencies. The VICTORS staff works in concert with employees, employers, and state and VA vocational agencies to keep individuals in the work force.

Screening procedures are often inadequate to determine whether an older individual's vision is suited to a particular job. Special problems may arise because older people fail to meet the prevailing vision screening standards that have been laid down as requirements for the job in question. This may lead to a person's being removed from the job or for the visual requirement's being waived.

Of all the criteria of visual performance, acuity is the simplest and the most widely used. As Michaels told conferees, it is true that the Snellen chart is poorly standardized, poorly calibrated, and sometimes poorly administered—but it is surprisingly reliable in detecting problems, and, after a century of use, it has maintained that reputation.

Bailey called attention to the fact that automated vision screeners have only one standard target luminance level, which might not be representative of the illuminance conditions at the job site. Instrumental vision screeners incorporate collections of tests that have usually been shown to be good at identifying visual capacities in young people. Many of the near-vision tests presented on instrumental vision screeners demand that the eye focus to a given close distance. The older person may not have a reading prescription adjusted for that particular distance. Furthermore, the near-vision distance chosen for the screener may not represent the working distance commonly used in the workplace. Ideally, every older person should have visual field record, according to Michaels, but sometimes this is not always practical. Visual field testing is recommended for any older person who gives headache as a primary complaint and who reports flashes, floaters, or curtains in the visual field. Although different parts of the visual field interact as a whole, central fields should be separated from peripheral fields in testing.

Donald Kline pointed out that as we learn more about the changes in the visual processing among older people and the significance of those changes for work performance, certain visual processes will logically emerge as candidates for testing. These include dynamic visual acuity and motion detection, visual field size, glare and glare recovery, distance perception, and visual search (which are taken up in a later section).

In summary, more information is needed regarding vision screening programs in U.S. companies. It is likely that visual acuity testing is the most widely used vision screening procedure in the work setting. While visual acuity testing serves an important role in measuring a certain aspect of visual performance, many other aspects of vision can and should addressed.

MATCHING WORKERS AND JOBS

Once the visual requirements of tasks are identified and suitable vision screening procedures are in place, appropriate job placement for all workers, including those with vision limitations, are essential. The Physical Placement Program of General Dynamics Corporation's Convair Division is an example of a program that strives to place workers in appropriate jobs through an elaborate coding system.

Physical placement codes are applied to employees with physical limitations to ensure that they are compatible with the assigned job classification, so that health problems will not be aggravated by the job and safe work conditions are provided for all employees. Alex reported to conferees:

> For instance, if a person has severe arthritis in his knees, he cannot, of course, be crawling around a fuselage drilling holes; he cannot climb ladders. If a person has a visual problem—monocular vision, let's say—we have a code for that. Everyone in our plant with monocular vision must wear either prescription or plano safety glasses. . . . We have areas where people are doing final assembly. We certainly want to make sure that those working in final assembly have depth and color vision. . . . We want to make sure they are not diabetic; we want to make sure they don't have epilepsy; we want to make sure that they don't have any tremors in their hand. We look at the whole person, but we do pay great attention to the eyes.

Table 2 provides a sample of the physical placement code definitions used by General Dynamics. The physical placement code assigned to an employee, according to Alex, signifies realistic physical limitations or potential hazards.

Such a system may well have application in many other job settings. The physical placement program described by Alex is not age-specific, although many medical problems that often accompany aging are probably captured by that system. In all likelihood,

TABLE 2 Example of Physical Placement Code Definitions

Category	Symbol	Definition
General Physical Capacity Code	U	Unlimited
	X	Worker must not lift or exert effort over 35 pounds
	Y	Worker must not lift or exert effort over 25 pounds
	Z	Worker must not lift or exert effort over 10 pounds
Specific Limitation or Restriction Code	1	Worker must wear safety glasses at all times while on company property
	1R	Worker must wear prescription lenses at all times while moving about on company property
	3	Worker's job must allow 40% sitting in performance of job tasks
	5	Worker must not be assigned work in which distance or depths must be judged accurately
	17	Worker must not work in position in which accurate color vision is essential

Based on Physical Placement Code Definitions, Convair Division, General Dynamics Corporation (R. Alex, 1986).

any physical placement program could be improved by the addition of visual screening procedures that more effectively capture job-relevant vision functions that change with age.

WORKPLACE DESIGN

The design of the workplace should allow workers, including those with vision problems, to perform required visual tasks efficiently and comfortably. In indoor office and factory workplaces, the major limitation on visual functioning typically results from a relative lack of illumination. As Kosnik pointed out, dimly lit environments may differentially impair performance of older workers. "The older worker's performance will be doubly compromised if small sized print, meters, labels, scales, or charts have to be read in poor or dim illumination." Localized, adjustable lighting for the work task can help older people by compensating for smaller pupil size. As Bailey pointed out, however, special care should be taken in providing extra illumination for older people so that glare is not introduced.

Roberta Alex reported that Convair's Safety Department performs lighting surveys at workstations when requested. Convair can accommodate visually impaired employees by providing supplemental lighting, magnification loops, or high magnification/high intensity portable inspection lamps. To illustrate further how Convair accommodates employees' vision needs, Alex described two case studies. In the first case, a 59-year-old man three years short of retirement developed diabetic retinopathy. The supervisor referred the employee to the medical services office; it was established that the employee was under the care of a retinal specialist. The company, in consultation with the employee and the union, placed the employee on permanent day shift to provide better lighting conditions. The firm also changed his job from drill press operator to machine parts finisher to eliminate work involving fine detail. In another case, a secretary who had been employed 19 years developed cataracts. She referred herself to medical services, according to Alex. She wanted to continue working for the six-month period preceding surgery. The action that was taken by the company was to provide the employee with a desk lamp and high intensity spotlight and to assign lengthy typing projects to other employees.

Another factor that may limit the performance of older workers is slowed processing of visual information, which manifests itself in a number of ways. According to Kosnik, "visual information that is scrolled on a video monitor may have to be displayed for a longer time in order to be read. Performance on externally paced visual tasks may show an age sensitivity that would be quite unexpected on the basis of ocular parameters alone." This is not to say that age-related changes in oculomotor parameters are not also of potential significance. For example, the vergence, pursuit, and vestibular-ocular response systems all may slow with aging and give rise to an apparent need for greater processing time.

Walsh added, however, that "differences in the duration of an internal representation of a particular visual display are likely to have relevance only for work situations associated with saccadic eye movement—such as reading or visual search. In most real-world viewing situations, the eye is free to select continued external input until perceptual recognition is complete." Walsh believes that everyday seeing is more affected by age differences in selective attention. "Consider the task of a person faced with way-finding in an urban environment. Present on the retina of the eye is a complex pattern of light containing sets of features for to-be-recognized landmarks, street signs, terrains, etc. In order to orient and direct themselves through this space, the person must scan and process a rich array of elements. Assuming that each element is recognized after it is selectively attended to in a sequential fashion, a slowing of attentional selection would work in a cumulative way to slow performance." The implication in the work setting, according to Walsh, might be evident in the work of a person operating complex equipment, a situation in which slowed selective attention may lead the operator to be unable to function adequately.

Changes in vision with age suggested to a number of conferees the need to consider training and retraining procedures for older workers. Czaja reported that the pervasiveness of computer technology means that many workers have had to learn to interact with computers on a daily basis. Czaja's research has shown that commercially available training strategies used to teach word processing are not effective for older learners. Czaja observed: "Perhaps even more basic are questions regarding the suitability of computer tasks for older persons. Few studies have examined whether there are age differences in task stress as a function of age of the operator. These are important issues, as the number of jobs involving computers will continue to increase, and this will impact on the employment status of older persons. Unless we develop effective retraining strategies, older persons will not fit into the new work environment."

If visual functioning is substantially reduced over time, especially due to disease, there are many changes that could be made in the workplace to keep workers with these problems on the job. It is useful to note that many individuals with macular disturbances often have an unusual need for strong illumination, according to Bailey, and that rather modest increases in illumination can sometimes have profound effects on visual performance.

In a paper prepared for the conference, Samuel Genensky pointed out that nearly all partially sighted people who have had appropriate visual aids prescribed, who are properly trained in the use of those aids, and who are motivated to use them, "can successfully perform such sight-intensive tasks as reading ordinary ink printed material, writing with a pen or pencil, moving about safely and alone in even an unfamiliar environment, and viewing a chalkboard or other distant display." The types of aids available to workers with limited sight are taken up in the next section.

Hilda Kahne told conferees that it is important that any efforts to increase the employabilitiy of workers include a consideration of changes in job design, such as part-time employment. Kahne observed, "I am not sure how much the availability of part-time work will solve the problem for the visually impaired," although there would seem to be a role, in her opinion.

In summary, although much remains to be learned, there is already considerable information available on visual processing changes that occur with age. The information in hand needs to be disseminated and discussed so that appropriate changes can be made eventually in the employment setting to benefit older workers.

RESPONDING TO THE VISION NEEDS OF OLDER WORKERS

Employers can save considerable time and money in building and sustaining a productive work force through health care and employment policies in which vision has been given a prominent role. In this section, we discuss what needs to be done to assist employers in improving or introducing programs that take into account the changes in vision that occur with age. In discussing procedures for responding to the vision needs of aging workers, we lay out the steps necessary to make vision screening, job placement, and environmental design suitable for the changes in vision that occur with age.

Estimating the Visual Requirements of Jobs

Employers motivated by safety considerations have developed a profile of the physical requirements of certain jobs, although the extent of that practice is not known. Information presented at the conference suggested that the visual performance characteristics identified by some employers—apart from acuity—include color vision and depth perception. While not age-specific, it is known that many of these visual characteristics are susceptible to age effects. Scientific findings on the visual processes that are susceptible to age effects and that are involved in visually guided tasks could help better identify visual requirements of jobs. This in turn might thereby enhance the employment of older workers. Corresponding to these other visual requirements are the age-sensitive visual skills of contrast sensitivity, glare and glare recovery, speed of visual processing, dynamic acuity, and night vision. Employers motivated by safety considerations and employers motivated by productivity concerns may eventually have at their disposal a framework for estimating the visual requirements of any job.

Vision Screening

Research suggests that workers engaged in visually guided tasks may experience a number of problems with their vision as they grow older. These problems may interfere with the performance of those tasks. Smaller pupil size and lens yellowing affect the amount of light reaching the retina. Loss of accommodative ability creates limitations on the range or working distances for which the eye can be used. Glare from uncontrolled light sources may present a problem, and slower visual processing speeds may make it more difficult for the older worker to deal with cluttered visual scenes, rapidly presented visual information, or detail (especially in conditions of poor illumination). Diseases affecting sight, furthermore, may substantially reduce the visual fields of older workers.

Although information is generally sketchy about the vision screening practices of American companies, it is probably the case that acuity testing is the most widely used screening procedure in preplacement and preemployment examinations of older workers. Depending on the visual requirements of the job, a number of vision screening procedures are recommended beyond acuity testing. Contrast sensitivity testing determines the threshold contrast required to detect objects (typically gratings) of varying spatial structure (spatial frequency). Acuity under low illumination can be measured using a variety of available techniques. Dynamic visual acuity is measured using acuity optotypes (such as Snellen letters), but under conditions in which these optotypes are moving and the observer must track them. The greatest drawbacks to the implementation of these procedures are: (1) the possible low feasibility of testing for these visual skills in preplacement or periodic screening examinations, given the time and/or sophistication of the equipment involved, and (2) the experimental nature of some of these procedures.

Job Placement

Once the vision requirements of the task have been specified and suitable vision screening procedures are available, employers and workers can benefit from the appropriate match between workers and jobs. Physical codes can be developed for certain jobs that spell out precisely the expected visual capacity of an employee to work at that job. While not age-specific, many of the visual performance characteristics that will have been identified will be those in which age-effects are known to occur and be measurable.

It was evident from the conference, however, that many visual skills that change with age can be compensated for—through adjustments in the design of the job, in the work environment, or through training. Hence, job placement procedures, practically speaking, may be used only in those situations in which a change in the task or the work environment is infeasible or the retraining of the worker is not advised for safety reasons.

Environmental and Job Design

Employers sensitive to the changing visual needs of older workers can improve the safety and productivity of workers in a variety of ways. For nondisease-related visual changes, the older worker may benefit from better illumination, more contrast in the material being used, reduced glare, larger print, and the like. If disease has led to more severe visual impairment, available options include part-time employment, job or task reassignment, or the provision of vision aids and retraining. Economists at the conference argued that special workplace accommodations that result in worker retention are more cost-effective in the long run.

2
Solutions

If employers know about or had access to the information reviewed at the conference, they would be able to improve or introduce programs that take into account the changing vision capabilities of their workers. The preceding section described work that needs to be done by the scientific and business communities before such programs can be put into place in their entirety.

But employers need not wait. There are many steps that could be taken now to improve the performance of workers based on current knowledge. This section identifies some of the possibilities raised by conference participants, which include providing suitable—sometimes very inexpensive—visual aids for older workers; providing opportunities for training and retraining on the job; raising illumination; introducing other selected modifications in the design of the work environment; adopting certain available screening procedures; and redesigning jobs. Taken separately or together, these actions could bring enormous returns to both workers and employers.

COMPENSATING FOR DECLINING VISUAL FUNCTION

In 1890 William James published a psychology text that even now, nearly a century later, contains many powerful insights. Among them is a proposed general law of perception: "Whilst part of what we perceive comes through our senses from the object before us, another part (and it may be the larger part) always comes out of our own mind."

Though one may not agree with James's claimed proportions—it may not be the larger part of perception that comes out of our own minds—it is hard to deny that the act of seeing draws on far more than just the neural information that is momentarily available from stimulating the eyes. A number of studies suggest that the past experiences that older people are able to draw on in the performance of certain tasks may overcome certain age effects in visual function. Practice is the principal agent creating important skill differences between experienced and inexperienced workers. And the expertise that comes with practice is certainly among the older worker's strong suits.

One such study, reported by Salthouse, examined transcription typing, that is, typing from printed copy.[6] This is an interesting activity from our current perspective because there is a large number of typists at many levels of experience at all ages, and typing is a perceptual-motor skill that laboratory results suggest declines with age. However, the Salthouse study yielded some surprising results.

Typists ranging from 19 to 72 years of age and with a range of typing speed from 17 to 104 net words per minute participated in a series of typing-like tasks. The sample was deliberately selected to result in a near-zero correlation between age and typing skill because the primary research question was not whether typing speed declined with age, but rather what were the differences between typists of different ages with the same overall level of skill.

Two of the initial measures obtained from each participant were the average time between successive keystrokes (interkey interval) while performing normal typing, and the average time between keystrokes while performing a standard reaction time task. These activities are structurally quite similar in that both involve rapid keystroke responses to visually presented alphabetic characters, but the stimuli in the choice reaction time task were presented discretely, with the next stimulus presented only after the response had been registered from the previous stimulus. The important finding to note from this study is that the age trends differ substantially for the two tasks despite considerable superficial similarity. Performance on the reaction time task exhibits

---

[6] Salthouse, T.A. (1984), Effects of age and skill in typing. *Journal of Experimental Psychology: General* 113:345–371.

quite typical age-related increases indicating poorer performance with increased age, yet performance of these same individuals on the typing task was virtually independent of age.

Subsequent manipulations in the project were designed to address two questions: (1) Why is there no age trend in the speed of typing when there is a pronounced age trend among the same individuals in the speed of responding in reaction time task? and (2) Why are people of all ages so much faster in their keystrokes in typing than in reaction time? Tentative answers to these questions came from a variation of the test, in which the number of preview characters in the display was systematically varied while typing; the average interkey interval was then measured as a function of the size of the preview window. The results indicate that average interval between keystrokes increases as the number of visible characters decreases below about 7 characters. This finding suggests that skilled typists begin processing characters to be typed well in advance of the current character. In fact, if only a single character is presented and typists are prevented from using this type of anticipatory processing, performance closely resembles that characteristic of the reaction time task. An examination of the age trends on these measures suggested to Salthouse that older typists employed a form of anticipatory processing to compensate for their slower perceptual-motor processes. This finding resembles those of Czaja.[7]

Other types of compensatory skills were described at the conference by Morgan:

> When I go from outdoors to indoors, it takes me much longer than anybody else in my group to find out what's going on. . . . I am relatively more certain that I don't see as well anyway, no matter how well I dark-adapt. I also notice that I have some difficulty separating blue colors. I can't tell sometimes whether the thing is lavender or pink. It so happens that in time I can arrive at the correct conclusion by introspection: if I am certain of the color, it's probably lavender; if I'm not certain, it's probably pink.
>
> I don't have as much trouble driving at night as one might think. Because I expect to have trouble driving at night, I have cut down my night driving. But I have great difficulty

---

[7] Czaja, S. and C. B. Drury (1981), Age and pretraining in industrial inspection. *Human Factors* 23:485–494.

driving at twilight. In part, it is due to the fact I have great difficulty in visual search, in finding the particular area—the scene—that I want to pick out that makes sense to me. I've gotten into the habit of taking a dry run to somebody's home that I have never visited before. I will drive to it in the middle of the afternoon to find out where it is, so that I won't get lost getting there in twilight.

The ability of older workers to develop compensatory skills and the role of practice should never be underestimated when considering visual changes among older workers.

BETTER VISION SCREENING PROCEDURES

Screening tests are often used to determine whether an individual's vision is adequate for a particular job. Vision screening procedures, however, are often not very job specific.

Kline reviewed a number of visual screening procedures that may be of interest to employers. In older workers, effective visual field size may be reduced, which argues for the inclusion of visual field tests in any screening procedure. At the present time, a few states require a visual field determination for a driver's license. As Michaels pointed out, every patient should have visual field records, but this is not always practical. As visual field extent is shown to be of importance in jobs involving visual search, for example, or in information-dense scenes, visual field testing may become more desirable and thus a standard part of screening procedures for older workers.

Many visual screening procedures that could be used by employers are still in the experimental phase. The contrast sensitivity function (CSF), for example, provides a more comprehensive statement of spatial vision abilities than do more traditional acuity measures, according to Kline. It does so by determining threshold contrast required to detect objects (typically gratings) by varying spatial structure (spatial frequency). It is likely that some work tasks depend more on intermediate spatial frequencies that are better assessed by the CSF than by standard acuity tests. Unfortunately, as Kline points out, although work is proceeding in this direction and test patterns are readily available, the diagnostic value of the CSF has yet to be demonstrated for such tasks.

Standard acuity testing gives little indication of a person's ability to distinguish detail in a rapidly moving object. More consideration should be given to tests to assess the visual fitness of older workers for tasks involving discrimination, such as occurs in driving or in "moving-part" industrial operations. Such standardized tests have yet to be developed, however.

As Michaels pointed out, the examination of the aging eye does not differ in essentials from that of any other eye except that it takes more time, more tact, and more patience. "It takes more time because older people frequently have many nonspecific complaints, poorly expressed, and sequentially muddled. Some symptoms may go unreported because of memory loss, fear, or indifference. It takes more tact because, in the nature of things, some senescent diseases are not only chronic but irreparable. It takes more patience because the aged eye often suffers multiple defects which must be sorted out." As more consideration is given to the introduction of more or different procedures to screen the visual capabilities of older workers, some thought will need to be given to the question of who will administer the tests and decide which tests are needed. A great deal of sensitivity should be applied in using procedures that may raise concerns about vision functions that heretofore have not been given much thought by most workers.

PROVIDING VISUAL AIDS

What simple changes might be made in the workplace in order to accommodate visually impaired workers? There are many simple magnification devices and techniques that can be put to use, such as a device to increase the relative size of the material to be used.

Bruce Rosenthal illustrated the point that it is possible to be quite clever in meeting people's vision needs:

> I would like to tell you what happened with one of my patients who is 84 years old. He was flying out to the West Coast to work on a case. He is a lawyer, and it was a $350 million case. He said, "I really would like to have some notes with me. What can I do? I don't want to use my lens because I have to hold it up very close." He really didn't want to use his high-powered lens because he didn't want to have anybody

look at him askance and think he really didn't know too much about the case. What we ended up doing was something very simple that everybody here can do. We got hold of one of the newer copiers which magnifies about 22 percent. We sent his notes through the copier once, a second time, then again. I think we did it about 20 times. He ended up with a few letters on 11" x 18" size paper. That solved his problem. He brought reams of paper into the courtroom, and he won the case.

Another technique involves moving the object toward the viewer's face, in effect, magnifying the image on the retina. There are high-powered reading spectacles that focus for a 16-inch working distance, although some people function much better using a hand magnifier. Stand magnifiers are devices that have plus lenses that are built into rigid housings. These are useful for arthritics or people who have a difficult time holding the lens steady, since the magnifier sits in a rigid housing.

Genensky, in a paper prepared for the conference, also identified the role of closed circuit television as a versatile visual aid currently available to partially sighted workers in some settings. Closed circuit television permits the control of the magnification of material seen on the screen as well as its brightness and contrast.

Simpler nonoptical aids are also available. The typoscope is certainly the simplest aid. This a piece of fairly stiff cardboard that is rectangular in shape and contains a rectangular slit or window in the middle. The typoscope is usually small enough to encompass all or a portion of a few lines of print when it is placed on a page. Morgan observed: "I very seldom find reported in the literature the problem of spatial interaction in reading printed material. It is the lack of border on the printed page as much as the fact that there is lack of space between the words and between the lines that makes it difficult to read. One of the solutions to the problem is a typoscope. . . . I need a white typoscope. I put it down on the paper, and I immediately increase the contrast between the print [and the background]. Now I have a nice, white background, which allows me to figure out the line of print."

In summary, many optical aids are available to augment declining sight.

RETRAINING OLDER WORKERS

The compensations older people make in response to declining sensory functioning suggest that learning, and therefore systematic training or retraining programs, could be helpful with respect to the visual performance of older workers. To what extent can training be used to improve performance directly through the development of compensatory strategies? Czaja reported at the conference that research has shown that appropriate training strategies can often enhance the task performance of older persons. Several studies have shown that a problem-solving discovery approach that minimizes rote memory is effective for older learners. It is also important to provide learners with immediate feedback to maximize the unlearning of incorrect responses and also to give them enough time to avoid deleterious pacing effects. Successful learning is important both in its own right and in helping to avoid negative attitudes that act as a barrier to the acquisition of new skills.

Learning and training are important areas to consider. And the issue of aging and training, which has not been examined very much from an industrial point of view, should be addressed from two different perspectives. The first is training in learning strategies. Czaja reported on evidence that suggests that the elderly are less likely to use cognitive strategies or learning strategies: "Things like mnemonic aids and mediators and organizing learning material. We have done some research on training older people to perform industrial inspection tasks. One thing we found was that providing them with pretraining on component skills that were relevant to the inspection task carried over later to subsequent inspection performance. We tried to provide pretraining and learning to learn kinds of skills, like organizing material, making size judgments, and the like."

The second perspective concerns how to train people for specific tasks. Czaja and her colleagues found that the success of older people in learning to perform new tasks or new jobs is highly dependent on the type of training method employed. "We certainly found this in our work when we looked at industrial inspection. We varied training. We used passive, traditional kinds of industrial approaches. We varied that with active, self-discovery feedback, and we found that this approach was superior. In fact, if people were provided with that kind of training, they could successfully learn to perform those tasks."

Czaja cautioned, however, that as people are being trained they are also forming attitudes about having to learn a new skill. "We did not find any age differences in attitude. We did find, however, that after training, people who reported a negative experience in the training session and who felt that they did poorly had a significant change in attitudes and were not too keen on using [the new skill]."

MODIFYING THE WORKPLACE

In indoor office and factory workplaces the major limitation on visual functioning of older workers results from a relative lack of illumination of the image on the retina. As Fozard reported to conferees, one study measured the time required by women in two age ranges from (19-27 years and 46-57 years) to complete a visual search task under three levels of illumination, 538, 1,076 and 1,614 lux. Performance times decreased with increasing levels of illumination in both age groups but more so for the older women. Other findings were that both groups expressed a preference for higher levels of illumination, and the older but not the younger women experienced greater eye comfort at the two higher levels.

Adequate illumination includes the ability to manipulate the lighting arrangement both to properly illuminate the object of visual attention and to control for glare. To achieve this it is necessary to provide workers with a degree of control over both general—usually ceiling—illumination as well as local illumination—usually lamps—of smaller areas. Provision of this degree of control is necessary but may not be sufficient, inasmuch as most people are accustomed to thinking of lighting in terms of a fixed entity, such as ceiling fixture or a piece of furniture, that should not be moved around simply for functional convenience. For these reasons the opportunity to manipulate lighting sources should be supplemented with some training designed to show people how to manipulate the visual environment to their advantage.

Environmental intervention can also mitigate the effects of age differences in adapting to changes in illumination. Changes that require shifts between very different levels of illumination can be especially difficult for older people. In raising light levels, however, it is important to avoid glare problems caused by creating excessive differences in brightness. One way to achieve this is to provide workers with individual control over both general and local illumination levels.

Video display terminals present special problems for the vision of older workers. With care, special glasses can be worn to bring the video screen to clearest focus for an individual, but commonly the keyboard and reference documents are located at other distances. So the individual working at a video display workstation must either accept blurred vision or change posture in order to view the keyboard or the reference documents. Thoughtful workplace design or the use of trifocals or progressive focal lenses can reduce these problems.

Working-distance problems are not just associated with video displays. Inspection of large diagrams or drawings, reference to large notice boards, and a multitude of various construction and manipulative tasks often require critical vision over a range of different viewing distances. Such tasks often present serious difficulties to older bifocal wearers who must change their head position or posture when they change their viewing from one object distance to another. Some of these problems are intrinsically unavoidable, but in many cases specially designed spectacle lenses or redesign of the work task can make work more comfortable and efficient.

Kosnik pointed out that dimly lit environments may differentially impair the performance of older workers. And older workers' performance will be doubly compromised if small-sized print, meters, labels, scales, charts, etc., have to be read in poor or dim illumination. Older workers may have more difficulty reading or locating targets when the visual scene is cluttered with other objects. As a result, visual acuity, assessed with one target at a time—or assessed with widely separated targets—may not provide an accurate guide to the functional acuity that the older worker brings to the job.

Pastalan offered a number of specific suggestions for enhancing the safety of older workers through appropriate environmental design. These include the use of sign systems that employ high contrast between symbol and background; the introduction of textured surfaces to reduce glare; the use of redundant cueing around machines and hazardous areas; the use of extreme contrasts in transitional zones (e.g., indoor-outdoor entrances); and the use of red-yellow colors where accents are required. Clearly, there is no shortage of ideas for changes that can be made in the workplace to facilitate the work of people with visual deficits.

JOB REDESIGN

Despite its demands, paid work is a critical component of adult life, and finding ways of extending a work attachment for the visually impaired as well as for other workers is very important. As Kahne pointed out, "Not only is it the customary source of economic support for individuals and their dependents, for many persons it makes possible valuable pension benefits and offers the only source of health insurance protection at reasonable cost prior to age 65. It often provides, as well, psychological support of 'community' and a sense of self-identity."

Can part-time work ever be a viable alternative to meet the needs of older workers for whom vision problems significantly impede the performance of their tasks? There is a lack of information to answer that question, but Kahne observed that institutional change to extend work attachment for the visually impaired will not be easy. Nonetheless, part-time employment may well be one of the more desirable approaches to responding to the employment needs of older workers whose declining vision has become a serious impediment to their employability.

3
Context for Change

The conference addressed the issue of keeping older workers in the work force longer, given the many changes that occur in vision with age. But, as Robinson pointed out, keeping older workers in the work force must be studied within the context of two opposing pressures. The first is the effect of government action to encourage the retention of older workers, which can be seen in the Age Discrimination in Employment Act amendments of 1978, recent changes in social security retirement benefit provisions, and the recent changes in mandatory retirement laws. The second and opposite pressure is the ongoing trend toward early retirement being fostered by the practices of business, labor, and older workers themselves. Attempts to extend working years by solving problems related to vision may be less than totally effective on a large scale if in fact working years are being reduced for reasons unrelated to vision.

We also need to look at the overall employability of people—their physical, and mental ability to perform a job. It is very important to understand how changes in vision relate to performance in the workplace in order to determine the job-person match.

In order to make it possible for workers to maintain their productivity despite declining visual functions and to remain employed (if they so wish) despite visual impairment, it will be necessary for scientists, employers, and different levels of government to form a partnership for change. Such a partnership would encourage scientists to pursue the research needed to provide elements in the design of an appropriate vision-based employment program. Employers might then have at their disposal the components for a program that would be sensitive to the vision needs of aging workers and suited to the tasks performed by their workers. The federal government could facilitate this academic-industrial exchange through its programs and policies. Each element of this three-part framework for change is taken up in the sections that follow.

THE POTENTIAL OF SCIENCE AND TECHNOLOGY

After many decades of research on the aging eye, the vision community is on the threshold of contributing significantly to the improvement of conditions surrounding the employment of older workers. Conferees described new directions for research to meet that challenge. These include increased emphasis on research related to basic visual processes for performing visually guided tasks, developmental or life-span research related to vision, research to promote suitable vision screening procedures for older workers, and further research on retirement decisions and employer practices. To the extent that manufacturers produce devices used by older workers on the job, they should emphasize the development of new technologies to meet the vision needs of older workers. Each of these goals is described in more detail in the pages that follow.

Research on Basic Visual Functions

A broad consensus emerged from the conference that the research system that has yielded so much information about the aging eye should be strengthened to promote the emergence of new information about the visual processes related to visually guided tasks. As suggested earlier in this report, such research might arise from a number of different quarters: survey analysis, laboratory research, on-site task analysis, and analysis using large statistical data bases. Emphasis should be placed on the identification of those aspects of vision that are involved in the performance of visually guided tasks and are susceptible to the effects of aging.

Life-Span Analysis

Although much information is available about normal visual processes, data are limited regarding the impact of basic changes in vision, such as reduced visual acuity, decreased powers of accommodation, increased sensitivity to glare, reductions in the visual field, and loss of color sensitivity on the performance of daily living activities or specific tasks such as visual inspection. In addition, data are limited regarding strategies that can be used to help compensate for the loss of visual performance. As Czaja told conferees, "We need to take a developmental view of design and allow for developmental changes which occur as a natural function of the aging process. Therefore we need data on the type and extent of these changes and their implications for the performance of everyday tasks and activities."

Life-span or developmental research can play an important role in understanding the subtle interaction between changes in vision with age and task performance. Life-span research may enable us to tease out the effects of experience from the effects of physiological changes in assessing worker performance of visually guided tasks and, as Walsh suggested, might also include an assessment of the differential effects of health and life-style in reducing the impact of age-related changes in vision on employment and performance. Expansion of developmental research to the area of work, aging, and vision might also have application in the training and retraining of older workers. As Czaja pointed out, the issue of training older workers has received little research attention historically:

> This is partially due to the commonly adhered to belief that because of changes in cognitive functioning, older people are resistant to or incapable of learning new tasks. Examination of the literature regarding aging and cognitive functioning suggests that there are age-related declines in efficiency of information processing. For example, most of the research examining memory functioning suggests that proficiency in remembering declines with age; deficits in primary memory appear to be marginal. Older persons also experience decline in perceptual ability; they have increased difficulty in dealing with complex or confusing stimuli. In addition, learning skills diminish or become rusty with age, and therefore the elderly are likely to have specialized needs.

The research results so far regarding training and aging are encouraging and suggest that given sufficient training, age-related differences in performance on some tasks can be minimized. Lifespan research could certainly contribute to this goal.

Research on Visual Screening Procedures

Vision screening may be a major event in the life of older workers: the results of vision tests can make the difference between being employed and not being employed or between doing the job one has always done or being reassigned to a new one. Furthermore, vision screening may point out visual problems that an older worker was completely unaware of—a phenomenon reported by Johnson. In Johnson's study (reported earlier), nearly 60 percent of all individuals tested who had visual field loss had no idea that they had a vision problem. As Michaels remarked to conferees, vision is a process that takes time, a factor usually ignored in practice—not because it is irrelevant but because there are no convenient clinical tests to measure it. "Dynamic visual acuity, flicker fusion frequency, perceptual span, reaction time, light adaptation, and masking are examples of theoretically important but clinically unexplored functions. Exceptions are time delay in optic nerve conduction manifest as the Marcus-Gunn pupil or the analogous Pulfrich phenomenon, time delay of glare recovery in macular disease, and the focusing time inertia patients complain of in early presbyopia."

Results from research on automobile driving provide the clearest indication of the types of screening procedures that might be suitable to estimate the visual capabilities of older workers. The issues associated with licensing, license revocation, insuring, and training/retraining older drivers provide a highly informative test bed for an examination of the broader issues associated with assisting older people in remaining productive in the workplace. As Kline pointed out, it has been estimated that over 90 percent of the information used in driving is visual; visual functions possibly related to accidents in which the driver was at fault include: limitations of acuity, contrast sensitivity, visual field, visual search, visibility due to poor illumination, inability to find information in the midst of visual clutter, and of course the interaction of these factors.

With some exceptions (for example, Johnson's research on visual fields), research attempts to relate visual functions to effective driving have not been particularly successful. This may be due to the fact that vision, although a major factor, is only one of many factors affecting driving performance, or that the tests used in research may measure visual characteristics not closely related to those used in driving. Kline told conferees:

> Still, a great deal can be done to enhance the efficacy of visual screening procedures, and research directed to this end is needed. Some research areas that appear to hold particular promise for developing more valid visual screening criteria for the older driver include: (1) visual search effectiveness as a function of driving condition and information load, (2) age differences in the visibility of signs as a function of type and spatial frequency characteristics at different luminance and contrast levels, (3) visual testing under high and low illumination conditions, (4) visual testing of the peripheral fields, using targets covering a range of sizes, luminances, and spatial density, (5) impact of veiling glare and photo-stress recovery on visual target identification, and (6) assessment of more dynamic or transient visual functions (including angular and in-depth motion sensitivity).

This research agenda may have application in the design of screening activities for older workers performing visually guided tasks other than driving.

Research on Factors Affecting the Retention and Retirement of Older Workers

The major factors that affect the degree of retention of older workers in the workplace may be classified into at least three categories: economic, social/psychological, and health/work capacity. Harold Sheppard told conferees that if these three broadly conceived factors are taken together, the ideal conditions for continued employment would consist of: a high demand for labor, inadequate pension expectation, rejection of public images associating chronological age with diminishing work capacities, high job satisfaction, aversion to lengthy full-time retirement, and good health.

Any attempt to improve the employment continuity of older workers, especially those with handicaps such as visual impairment, must go beyond the levels associated with these conditions, according to Sheppard. "What is required are special interventions ranging from education and persuasion of employers, unique labor-management agreements, tailor-made training techniques, to creative technologies that facilitate the workability of the handicapped." Sheppard suggested that we need to learn such things as:

(a) What special arrangements and adaptations, if any, can be made to facilitate employment?
(b) Are there empirical data that can shed light on the relative cost-effectiveness of such practices, with special care taken to encompass all costs and benefits, including social costs and benefits as well as those experienced by the employer or employee?
(c) What transfers and adaptations from ergonomic job-related technologies can be applied to improving the employment of the visually impaired? How much has been put into practice already, and how could information about this be effectively disseminated?
(d) Related to the above, what are some of the cost-effectiveness considerations?
(e) Many companies in manufacturing industries have employed "handicapped" workers—industries that have subsequently been experiencing severe work force lay-offs and shutdowns. What is the labor market and job hunting experience of "handicapped" workers who have been laid off, relative to the displaced workers as a whole? What factors are associated with success in finding jobs?
(f) What are the attributes of organizations, beyond the typically examined ones such as industry characteristics, that form a basis for hiring or retaining older workers in general? Impaired ones in particular?

The answer to these and related questions may help to determine those policies and practices that meet the needs of both employers and older workers.

Research on Technological Change

Research will yield answers to many questions regarding the role of vision functions that change with age and worker performance. The results of those research efforts can be expected to have application in a wide variety of ways—in the use of more relevant vision screening procedures for older workers, in appropriate job design and job placement, and in the design of a more efficacious working environment. Research and development activities to understand visual functions that change with age should also be pursued by those companies responsible for the design of equipment used by older workers. Such activities might prevent the exacerbation of problems associated with declining visual functions among older workers.

For example, portable work units might permit the adjustment of lighting levels by older workers to suit individual needs; more contrast between symbols and background might be added to the manufacturers of keyboards or panels.

Similarly, those manufacturers engaged in the production of corrective devices (visual prosthetics) may wish to pay special attention to the visual needs of older workers, if they have not done so already.

As Arnold Small told conferees, "The consideration of workstation design includes the effective matching of machine and environment compatibly with older worker characteristics including vision. The environment includes warnings, instructions, and visual communication overall"—clearly indicating a proper role for equipment manufacturers in meeting the needs of older workers.

EMPLOYER COMMITMENT AS A CRITICAL ELEMENT FOR CHANGE

Most employers are not looking for ways to retain older workers. So, in proposing that they redesign workstations or jobs to meet the visual needs of older workers, we should not be surprised to find that such proposals are met with a cool reception.

Do most employers encourage retirement? Yes: at least larger firms tend to, according to Robinson. Pension plans often subsidize early retirement. "One major study found that 75 percent of the pension plans analyzed offered a fully accrued pension at some early retirement date. Many plans provide a supplemental benefit until the age of eligibility for social security. In some plans, normal retirement age is considerably below age 65. A combination of age plus service, commonly age 55 and 10 years of service, is frequently used for pension eligibility."

Why do employers encourage early retirement? Some companies are bound by early retirement provisions in union contracts. Other companies, according to Robinson, cite a combination of reasons: the higher salaries related to length of service, the relatively high cost of benefits, declining performance of older employees (identified by 37 percent of chief executives in one survey as their companies' greatest concern about older workers), skill obsolescence, and the like.

Given the seemingly inexorable trend to early retirement in many companies, strategies to promote work-life extension through overcoming vision problems need to be targeted to those kinds of organizations and to those segments of the work force in which either retention of older workers or the rehiring of retirees is recognized as an economic advantage.

Since policies regarding the utilization of older workers depends in part on employer perceptions of the relationship between age and job performance, Parnes observed that it is obvious that negative perceptions function as a disincentive among employers to retain or to hire older people. Employers must be made more aware of the weak association between age and work performance—and the importance of making decisions based on individuals, not age categories. Skill obsolescence as an inexorable phenomenon is deeply entrenched in the thinking of most of us, and it requires a healthy skepticism as to just how unavoidable it is. Greater attention is needed to the extent to which skill obsolescence occurs because of managerial policy and employee motivation and what are the interventions that can effectively correct it, including appropriately designed training and retraining approaches. Training and retraining are frequently resisted on the part of employers on grounds of poor cost-effectiveness (as well as stereotypes about age and learning).

Some employers are sensitive to the prospect that training a 50-year-old may also be more cost-effective than training a much younger person, given the data on higher turnover among young employees. The greater reliability of older workers could be an incentive to employers for retaining individual older workers.

FEDERAL PROGRAMS AND POLICIES

A basic challenge for policy research in this field is to ascertain and disseminate those policies and practices that meet the needs of both employers and older workers. It may be asking too much of employers simply to adapt—in a unidirectional fashion—to the needs of workers.

How does all this relate to federal concerns? According to McConnell, public policy can have a great influence on the retention of older workers in the labor force. Since there are a number of interests involved, public policy necessarily has the task of balancing these interests.

The question has been raised whether certain occupations should be exempted from the Age Discrimination and Employment Act (ADEA) of 1967, which generally prohibits discrimination in personnel practices on the basis of age except "where age is a bona fide occupational qualification (BFOQ) reasonably necessary to the normal operation of the particular business." Recent Supreme Court decisions indicate that the BFOQ is a very narrow exception to the general rule that age discrimination is unlawful. Age as a BFOQ can be shown in one of two ways. An employer can attempt to demonstrate that all or substantially all persons over age 40 would be unable to perform a given job effectively or safely. Alternatively, age can be used as a BFOQ if it is related to safety and it would be "impossible or highly impractical" to measure safety-related attributes on an individual basis. This two-part inquiry has been accepted by every Court of Appeals, the Equal Employment Opportunity Commission, Congress, and the Supreme Court when a BFOQ defense has been raised by an employer.

Gerald Barrett discussed the problem of age discrimination in employment in terms of the example of commercial drivers. An employer defending age as a BFOQ for commercial drivers because it is "impossible or impractical" to measure individual safety-related attributes must take a sequential three-part approach. First, the employer must show that older commercial drivers have more accidents than their young counterparts. (This does *not*, however, seem to be the case.) Second, the employer must demonstrate that there are no individually valid tests that predict accident involvement. Research, however, suggests that some tests, including those that assess perceptual style, auditory selective attention, dynamic visual acuity, and acuity under low illumination might be used for this purpose. Third, the employer must show that age is related to accident involvement but that it is "impractical" to use a valid test. It would be necessary to demonstrate either that age is not strongly related to a valid test or that it is not practical to use the valid test for selection. Wide individual differences in test performance do not imply that a higher proportion of older adults would not fail a valid predictor of accident involvement. But at least the test, and not age as its proxy, would serve as the selection device.

Legislative protection for older workers is also provided by the Job Training Partnership Act. If older workers with physical impairments are to be retained in the labor force, it would be desirable to expand this program. Older workers might have to learn to use new forms of visual information or may have to learn a job with fewer visual demands.

Finally, public policy on benefits, which has a great influence on age of retirement, is open to modification. The decision to require keeping an employee over 65 on company health plans has meant increased cost for employers. The situation is complex because reversing that decision, while benefiting employers, would increase Medicare costs.

In summary, there are a number of legislative policies that could inadvertently compete with efforts to retain older workers in the work force longer, given changes that occur in vision naturally with age or through disease. A more systematic analysis of these policies than that provided by the conference would be helpful in opening the way for modifications in the employment conditions of older workers described in this report.

CONCLUSION

The aging of the human eye involves a series of changes in visual performance that can be readily detected in the healthy adult. Viewed in the context of employment, reduced visual functioning need not have any effect on job performance. But for some individuals it will. It is obviously in the employer's interest to be responsive to the visual needs of older workers—indeed, of all workers. A firm may save considerable time and money in building and sustaining a productive work force through health care and employment policies in which vision has been given a prominent role. Evidence suggests that much has already been done by some firms to meet the vision needs of their workers. But much more work lies ahead.

In order to make it possible for all workers to maintain their productivity in the face of changes in vision that typically occur with age, it will be necessary for scientists, manufacturers, and employers to pursue some common goals. Scientists will need to give more emphasis to research which promotes suitable vision screening procedures for older workers, for example, and leads to a better understanding of the normal changes that occur in vision over the course of person's life. To the extent that manufacturers produce the devices used by older workers at the job site, attention should be given to the development of new technologies or improvements in existing technologies to meet the vision needs of older workers. Portable work units might permit the introduction of appropriate lighting levels by older workers, for example, and keyboards and panels offer greater contrast between symbols and their backgrounds than is presently found to benefit older—if not all workers.

Once advances such as these have been made, employers might then have at their disposal the components for a vision-based employment program which would be sensitive to the vision needs of aging workers and suited to the unique tasks performed by all workers.

Appendix A
Conference Participants and Program

Participants

ROBERTA ALEX, Medical Services, General Dynamics Corporation, San Diego, Calif.
IAN BAILEY, School of Optometry, University of California, Berkeley
GERALD BARRETT, Department of Psychology, University of Akron
LOUISE BIRKHOLZ, Medical Aid Office, S&C Electric Company, Chicago, Ill.
RICHARD BURKHAUSER, Department of Economics, Vanderbilt University
SARA CZAJA, Department of Industrial Engineering, State University of New York, Buffalo
STEVEN FERRIS, New York University School of Medicine*
JAMES FOZARD, Gerontology Research Center, National Institute on Aging
ROBERT GOTTSDANKER, Department of Psychology, University of California, Santa Barbara*
CHRIS JOHNSON, Department of Ophthalmology, University of California, Davis
HILDA KAHNE, Department of Economics, Wheaton College
CORINNE KIRCHNER, Research Division, American Foundation for the Blind, New York
DONALD KLINE, Department of Psychology, University of Notre Dame*

---

*Member, Working Group on Aging Workers and Visual Impairment

WILLIAM KOSNIK, Department of Psychology, Northwestern University
ALAN LEWIS, Department of Vision Sciences, State University of New York, State College of Optometry, New York
JOSEPH MAINO, Eye-VICTORS Clinic, Kansas City VA Medical Center
STEPHEN McCONNELL, Special Committee on Aging, United States Senate
DAVID MICHAELS, Department of Ophthalmology, University of California, Los Angeles*
MEREDITH MORGAN (emeritus), School of Optometry, University of California, Berkeley*
LEON PASTALAN, Department of Architecture and Urban Planning, University of Michigan
PAULINE ROBINSON (formerly), Andrus Gerontology Center, San Francisco
BRUCE ROSENTHAL, Department of Vision Sciences, State University of New York, State College of Optometry, New York
TIMOTHY SALTHOUSE, Department of Psychology, University of Missouri, Columbia
ROBERT SEKULER, Cresap Neuroscience Laboratory, Northwestern University*
HAROLD SHEPPARD, International Exchange Center on Gerontology, University of South Florida
ARNOLD SMALL (emeritus), Department of Human Factors, University of Southern California
DAVID WALSH, Department of Psychology, University of Southern California
RONALD WILSON, Division of Epidemiology and Health Promotion, National Center for Health Statistics

Observers

RAY BRIGGS, Institute of Safety and Systems Management, University of Southern California
DAN FIFE, Insurance Institute for Highway Safety, Washington, D.C.
WILLIAM FREEDMAN, National Science Foundation
HOWARD HANNA, Office of Highway Safety, Federal Highway Administration

LEONARD JAKUBCZAK, National Institute on Aging
SOL LANDAU, Midlife Services Foundation, Miami
BERNARD E. NASH, Worker Equity Department, American Association of Retired Persons, Washington, D.C.
CYNTHIA NULL, Federation of Behavioral, Psychological and Cognitive Sciences, Washington, D.C.
L. DENO REED, National Institute on Disability and Rehabilitation Research, Washington, D.C.
FRED ROYER, VA Medical Center, Brecksville, Ohio
STEVEN SANDELL, National Commission for Employment Policy, Washington, D.C.
MICHAEL SLOANE, Department of Psychology, University of Alabama
JOAN STELMACK, Blind Rehabilitation Center, Hines Veterans Hospital, Illinois
LAETITIA STOCK, National Society to Prevent Blindness, New York
JOSEPH F. STURR, Psychology Department, Syracuse University
THOMAS TRECIDI, USAF School of Aerospace Medicine, Brooks AFB, Texas
DAVID WORTHEN, Veterans Administration

CONFERENCE ON WORK, AGING, AND VISION

February 25 and 26, 1986

The Lecture Room
National Academy of Sciences
Washington, D.C.

Tuesday, February 25

8:30 a.m.	Welcome	Robert Sekuler
	Invited remarks	David Worthen Veterans Administration
		Leonard Jakubczak National Institute on Aging

9:00 a.m. Panel 1: Relationships Between Vision and Age

What happens to the eye with age; some relationships between visual changes with age and changes in behavior; impact of visual deficits on cognitive functions; relationship of visual changes with age to other health changes; coping strategies.

William Kosnik	Leon Pastalan
David Michaels	Robert Sekuler
Meredith Morgan	David Walsh

11:00 a.m. Break

11:15 a.m. Panel 2: Changing Demographics of the U.S. Labor Force: Vision, Age and Work

Incidence and prevalence of visual impairment with age; health status factors in leaving the work force; demographic changes in the U.S. work force.

Richard Burkhauser	Stephen McConnell
Hilda Kahne	Pauline Robinson
Corinne Kirchner	Ronald Wilson

1:00 p.m. Luncheon

2:30 p.m.   Panel 3: Vision, Age and Human Performance

Effects of visual changes with age on job skills, problems of performance assessment; driving as a special example; bona fide occupational qualifications.

James Fozard   Chris Johnson
Sara Czaja   Gerald Barrett
Donald Kline   Timothy Salthouse

5:00 p.m.   Cocktails

6:00 p.m.   Dinner

Wednesday, February 26

9:00 a.m.   Panel 4: Keeping Older Americans in the Work Force Longer

Screening practices; providing visual prosthetics; job redesign/task redesign; work station redesign; economic incentives/disincentives.

Roberta Alex   Joseph Maino
Ian Bailey   Bruce Rosenthal
Louise Birkholz   Harold Sheppard
Alan Lewis   Arnold Small

Noon   Luncheon

2:00 p.m.   Overview   Steven Ferris
                                   Robert Gottsdanker
                                   Robert Sekuler

2:30 p.m.   General discussion

4:00 p.m.   Adjournment

Appendix B
Annotated Bibliography

This bibliography has been designed to provide interested individuals with a list of further readings on the effects of aging on human visual function and the relationship of those effects to work performance. The bibliography is not intended to serve as a comprehensive list of readings in this area; rather, it serves as a mechanism to orient readers to the diverse literature comprising this area.

The bibliography is divided into five major sections: (1) basic visual changes with age; (2) age changes in higher-level perceptual processes; (3) the impact of vision on work; (4) low vision and optical aids; and (5) general texts on vision and aging. The third section, "Impact of Vision on Work," is further subdivided into 3 sections: (1) employment status; (2) task performance; and (3) environmental design.

Each annotation briefly describes the major foci of the book or article. When the item being annotated is a general text, the annotation highlights the content of the reference specifically related to work, aging, and vision.

BASIC VISUAL CHANGES WITH AGE

Kline, D. W., and Schieber, F. J.
    1985   Vision and aging. Pp. 296–331 in J. E. Birren and K. W. Schaie, eds., *Handbook of the Psychology of Aging*. New York: Van Nostrand Reinhold.

This chapter is a basic review of the changes that occur in vision with aging. It includes information on changes in the eye and brain, visual pathologies, light sensitivity, color vision, spatial resolution, temporal resolution, and higher-level perceptual processes.

Michaels, D. D.
- 1985 *Visual Optics and Refraction: A Clinical Approach.* St. Louis: The C. V. Mosley Company.

Textbook on optics and refraction that includes a chapter on refraction of the aging eye. This chapter describes structural and functional changes of the aging eye and discusses the diagnosis and treatment of presbyopia. Also includes a chapter on prescribing low vision aids.

- 1986 Ocular disease in the aged. Pp. 135–167 in A. A. Rosenbloom, Jr., and M. W. Morgan, eds., *Vision and Aging: General and Clinical Perspectives.* New York: Professional Press Books/Fairchild Publications.

Presents an overview of the aging eye and its clinical evaluation. Reviews the features of several age-related ocular diseases, including diseases of the orbit, cornea, lens, retina, and optic nerve. Also reviews the ophthalmic signs of diseases, such as arteriosclerosis, diabetes, and hypertension.

National Center for Health Statistics
- 1978 *Refractive Status and Mobility Defects of Persons 4–74 Years, United States, 1971–1972.* Prepared by J. Roberts and M. Rowland. Vital and Health Statistics. Series 11, Number 206. DHEW Pub. No. (PHS) 78-1654. Washington, D.C.: U.S. Department of Health, Education, and Welfare.

Reports estimates on refraction status, maximum corrected visual acuity, and eye motility defects among the civilian noninstitutionalized population in the United States. These estimates, based on findings from the ophthalmology examination in the Health and Nutrition Examination Survey of 1971–1972, are analyzed with respect to several demographic and socioeconomic variables.

- 1983 *Eye Conditions and Related Need for Medical Care Among Persons 1–72 Years of Age: United States, 1971–1972.* Prepared by J. Ganley and J. Roberts. Vital Health Statistics, Series 11, No. 228. DHHS

Pub. No. (PHS) 83-1678. Washington, D.C.: U.S. Department of Health and Human Services.

Contains estimates of the total prevalence of various types of eye abnormalities and vision decrease from abnormal conditions among the civilian noninstitutionalized population of the United States. Based on findings from the ophthalmology examination in the National Health and Nutrition Examination Survey of 1971-1972 and analyzed with respect to various demographic and socioeconomic factors.

    1984   *Eye Care Visits and Use of Eyeglasses or Contact Lenses, United States, 1979 and 1980.* Vital and Health Statistics. Series 10, No. 145. DHHS Pub. No. (PHS) 84-1573. Washington, D.C.: U.S. Department of Health and Human Services.

Presents national estimates of volume and frequency of eye care visits and types of eye care professionals seen, based on data collected in 1979 by the National Health Interview Survey. Also reports on the use of eyeglasses and contact lenses in 1979 and 1980 and on trends in corrective lenses since 1966.

Weale, R. A.
    1982   *A Biography of the Eye: Development, Growth, Age.* London: H. K. Lewis & Co. Ltd.

Examines ocular aging in a developmental framework. Discusses ocular embryology and the properties of the infant eye. Chapters are devoted to detailed discussions of the effects of aging on the eyeball, the uveal tract, the crystalline lens, the retina, and the brain. Summarizes data on visual capabilities such as acuity, contrast sensitivity, and temporal resolution as a function of age.

AGE CHANGES IN HIGHER-LEVEL PERCEPTUAL PROCESSES

Kline, D. W., and Schieber, F. J.
    1982   Visual persistence and temporal resolution. Pp. 231-244 in R. Sekuler, D. Kline, and K. Dismukes, eds., *Aging and Human Visual Function.* New York: Alan R. Liss, Inc.

Discusses factors contributing to the loss with age in the temporal resolving power of the visual system. Critically reviews the evidence suggesting that stimulus persistence effects in the nervous system account for the loss of temporal resolution. Points to one need for further research in the area.

Sekuler, R., and Owsley, C.
    1982   The spatial vision of older humans. Pp. 185–202 in R. Sekuler, D. Kline, and K. Dismukes, eds., *Aging and Human Visual Function.* New York: Alan R. Liss, Inc.

Discusses measurement of the contrast sensitivity function as a method of assessing spatial vision integrity. Presents contrast sensitivity data for younger and older observers, which indicate sensitivity losses at intermediate and high spatial frequencies for older adults. Studies relating these losses to age differences in human face perception are reported. Data on age differences in motion sensitivity are also presented.

Walsh, D. A.
    1982   The development of visual information processes in adulthood and old age. Pp. 204–230 in R. Sekuler, D. Kline, and K. Dismukes, eds., *Aging and Human Visual Function.* New York: Alan R. Liss, Inc.

Examines age differences in visual functioning in the framework of visual information processing models. Describes these models and the distinctions drawn between peripheral and central perceptual processes. Reviews the results of experiments demonstrating that older adults are slower than young adults in more than one stage of visual information processing.

IMPACT OF VISION ON WORK

Employment Status

Kahne, H.
    1985   *Reconceiving Part-time Work: New Perspectives for Older Workers and Women.* Totowa, N. J.: Rowan & Allanheld.

Discusses the demographic, economic, and societal trends that influence work patterns. Finds that part-time work schedules will become increasingly important in the future and suggests how currently employed part-time work arrangements can be improved. Examines the interests and needs of women and older workers in part-time work and the impact of social policies and legislation on part-time work for older workers. Explores the influence of unions' and employers' opinions and policies on part-time work structure and availability. Impacts of visual function are not considered. Includes an extensive bibliography on older workers and employment.

National Commission for Employment Policy
    1985   *Older Worker Employment Comes of Age: Practice and Potential.* Washington, D.C.: National Commission for Employment Policy

Guide to various aspects of older worker employment. Includes discussions on who the older worker is, work arrangements for older workers, policies affecting older workers, and initiatives in the employment sector to help older workers find and retain jobs. Does not deal specifically with visual impairment.

U.S. Congress, Senate
    1985   *Health and Extended Worklife.* Special Committee on Aging. Prepared by D. D. Newquist. Washington, D.C.: U.S. Government Printing Office.

This document presents health status information on older persons as it relates to extending their work lives. Summarizes data from the National Center for Health Statistics and the Social Security Administration on various health and disability measures of middle-aged and older populations. Discusses these data in the broad context of health, aging, and work. Several areas of research need are listed.

Office of Technology Assessment
    1985   *Technology and Aging in America.* Washington, D.C.: U.S. Government Printing Office.

Discusses the impact of technology on several aspects of the functional status of the older person, such as health, living environments, and employment. Reviews demographic trends in the United States and considers how advances in technology affect employment opportunities for older workers. Discusses the costs and benefits of job retraining programs for older workers. Also discusses the use of technology to improve worker health and safety and to assist older workers with physical impairments. Includes an appendix that lists devices used by workers with physical or sensory deficits, including visual impairments.

Paul, C. E.
    1983   *A Human Resource Management Perspective on Work Alternatives for Older Workers.* Washington, D.C.: National Commission for Employment Policy.

Survey of 25 companies known for progressive programs addressing the needs of older workers. Discusses the forms these programs take, the variables that influence management's decision on whether to implement such programs, the extent to which the programs are used by older workers, and the impacts of public policies on the development of such programs. No discussion of how such programs might address visual impairments.

Robinson, P. K.
    1983   *Organizational Strategies for Older Workers.* New York: Pergamon Press.

Reviews the literature on management strategies for an aging work force. Contains several annotations of references in the field as well as a recommended reading list.

Robinson, P. K., Livingston, J. L., and Birren, J. E., eds.
    1984   *Aging and Technological Advances.* New York: Plenum Press.

Proceedings from a symposium sponsored by the NATO Special Program Panel on Human Factors. Presents a broad view of the positive and negative consequences of technology for the aging. Includes chapters on labor force participation, health and stress, human factors, home and community. Several chapters consider issues relevant to the older worker's employment status. Includes a limited amount of material related specifically to technology and visual impairment in the aging.

Root, L. S., and Zarrugh, L. H.
    1983   *Innovative Employment Practices for Older Americans.* Washington, D.C.: National Commission for Employment Policy.

Analyzes a variety of programs and practices initiated by companies to create employment options for older workers. Descriptions of companies were obtained from the National Older Worker

Information System (NOWIS), a computerized data base. Programs and practices include part-time work assignments, job training/retraining, and job redesign. With rare exceptions, the programs do not address visual needs of the older worker.

U.S. Congress, Senate
> 1985 *Personnel Practices for an Aging Work Force: Private-Sector Examples.* Special Committee on Aging. Prepared by L. S. Root and L. H. Zarrugh. Washington, D.C.: U.S. Government Printing Office.

This paper is based on the National Older Worker Information System (NOWIS), a data base of practices and programs in the private sector that can benefit older workers. Discusses part-time employment practices, training programs, and job redesign initiatives. Summaries of 38 company programs selected from the data base are presented. Physical redesign of the workstation to accommodate disabilities such as visual impairment is an uncommon practice among the sample companies.

> 1986 *Aging America: Trends and Projections.* Special Committee on Aging. Washington, D.C.: U.S. Government Printing Office.

This document presents a general overview of the size, growth, and geographic distribution of the older population, as well as data on its health, income, employment, housing, and social status.

Task Performance

Davison, P. A.
> 1985 Inter-relationships between British drivers' visual abilities, age and road accidents. *Ophthalmic and Physiological Optics* 5:195–204.

An analysis is provided of 1,000 drivers' accident histories on a vision screening instrument. Significant relationships were seen between various accident variables and several different vision tests. Retesting drivers' vision at about age 50 was recommended.

Evans, D. W., and Ginsburg, A. P.
> 1985 Contrast sensitivity predicts age-related differences in highway-sign discriminability. *Human Factors* 23(6): 637–642.

Examines whether contrast sensitivity measurements can be used to predict age-related differences in the ability to discriminate simple highway signs. Snellen visual acuity and contrast sensitivity measures were determined for a group of younger observers (ages 19 to 30) and group of older observers (ages 55 to 79). Although visual acuity was the same in the two groups, the younger observers were able to discriminate road signs at significantly greater distances than the older observers. The results of the discrimination experiment correlated well with contrast sensitivity measures at 1.5 and 12 cycles per degree.

Holmes, C., Tolliffe, H., Gregg, J., Cameron, I., and Blyth, R.
    1958   *Guide to Occupational and Other Visual Needs*, Volume 1. Los Angeles: Silver Lake Lithographers, Inc.

Presents an analysis of the visual tasks involved in several occupations and avocations. This classic volume was motivated to a large degree by a concern for prescribing proper lenses to give presbyopes clear vision at multiple working distances. Each analysis describes the workstation in terms of locations of work areas and working distances. The analyses comment on the requirements for visual acuity, ocular motility, depth perception, peripheral vision, and color discrimination and also discuss other factors affecting lens prescription, such as lighting and safety.

Institute of Medicine
    1981   *Airline Pilot Age, Health and Performance: Scientific and Medical Considerations.* Washington, D.C.: National Academy Press.

Report of the Committee to Study Scientific Evidence Relevant to Mandatory Age Retirement for Airline Pilots. Provides a comprehensive review of information regarding how advances in age may impact the ability of airline pilots to perform their jobs safely. The report includes a consideration of the pilot's job, safety and methodological issues, age-related health changes, perceptual and psychomotor changes with age, and alternative approaches to the evaluation of pilot proficiency.

Panek, P. E., Barrett, G. V., Sterns, H. L., and Alexander, R. A.
    1977   A review of age changes in perceptual information processing ability with regard to driving. *Experimental Aging Research* 3(6):387–449.

Reviews age-related changes in vision, hearing, and information processing abilities, such as selective attention and perceptual-motor reaction time, as they impact driving behavior. Includes an extensive reference list.

Salthouse, T. A., and Somberg, B. L.
    1982   Skilled performance: Effects of age and experience on elementary processes. *Journal of Experimental Psychology: General* 111(2):176–207.

Examines the effects of practice on the performance of four simple tasks by younger adults (ages 19-27) and older adults (ages 62-73). Tasks included are signal detection, memory scanning, visual discrimination, and temporal prediction. Findings indicate that practice improves performance in both age groups, but that age differences remain. Suggests that differences between young and old in performance of simple perceptual and cognitive tasks are due to a slower overall rate of information processing.

Sekuler, R. S., Kline, D., and Dismukes, K., eds.
    1982   Aging and visual function of military pilots: A review. *Aviation, Space, and Environmental Medicine* 53(8):747–758.

Report of Working Group 55 of the Committee on Vision. Summarizes the visual tasks of pilots and reviews the visual functions crucial to the performance of these tasks, emphasizing the effects of age on these functions. Discusses methodological obstacles to determining the effects of age on visual function and performance of visual tasks. Presents recommendations for further research.

Sivak, M., Olson, P. L., and Pastalan, L. A.
    1981   Effect of driver's age on nighttime legibility of highway signs. *Human Factors* 23(1):59–64.

Examines the relationship between driver's age and nighttime legibility of highway signs. Findings show that the distances required to correctly read a sign for older drivers (over age 61) are 65 to 77 percent of those for younger drivers (under age 25). Suggests that legibility standards should not be based solely on data from the young and that standard (high luminance) acuity tests may be poor predictors of nighttime visual performance.

Welford, A. T.
1976   Thirty years of psychological research on age and work. *Journal of Occupational Psychology* 49:129-138.

Historical review of research in industrial gerontology in Britain beginning in 1946. Summarizes the main ideas that emerged from this research and discusses future research needs in the area of aging and work.

Environmental Design

Boyce, P. R.
1981   *Human Factors in Lighting.* New York: MacMillan Publishing Co., Inc.

Comprehensive survey of the impact of lighting conditions on people's responses. Reviews fundamentals of the quantification and production of light and basic information on vision. Examines the relationship between lighting and work. Explores people's reactions to different lighting conditions, along dimensions such as discomfort, and discusses the standards, codes, and guides for specification of lighting in different environments. Presents a brief review of the effects of age on visual performance as determined by such basic measures as visual acuity (pp. 231-248).

Guth, S. K., Eastman, A. A., and McNelis, J. F.
1956   Lighting requirements for older workers. *Illuminating Engineering* 30:656-660.

Classic study of the effect of age on visibility levels. Observers were office and laboratory workers ranging in age from 17 to 65. Measurements of word recognition were made in illumination levels varying from 10 to 100 footcandles. Results indicate an increase in lighting requirements with increasing age.

Fozard, J. L.
1981   Person-environment relationships in adulthood: Implications for human factors engineering. *Human Factors* 23(1):7-27.

Discusses designing environments for the aging and the elderly. Reviews the literature on the effects of aging on vision, hearing, the other senses, learning, memory, health, and work variables. Discusses human factors interventions for those changes that occur with age.

Hakkinen, L.
1984   Vision in the elderly and its use in the social environment. *Scandanavian Journal of Social Medicine* Supplement 35:1–60.

Study of the visual function and visual requirements of daily life in the elderly, based on data from 601 residents of Turku, Finland, age 65 and older. Reports measurements of visual functions such as best corrected visual acuity, color vision, visual field, grating acuity, and contrast sensitivity. The study also explores the relationship between visual functions and social data such as living arrangements and the needs for vision in daily activities. Includes a review of the literature and 303 references.

Hughes, P.
1981   Lighting for the elderly: A psychobiological approach to lighting. *Human Factors* 23(1):65–85.

Reviews the literature on the role of illumination in optimizing indoor environments for the elderly, emphasizing both the impact of illumination on vision and the photobiological effects of light. Discusses physiological changes that occur with aging and the effects of aging on visual performance. Comments on good lighting design practices for different environments, including the work environment.

Kaufman, J. E., and Haynes, H., eds.
1981   *IES Lighting Handbook*. New York: Illuminating Engineering Society of North America.

This technical handbook of light and its applications is published in two comprehensive volumes, a reference volume and an application volume. The reference volume includes chapters on the physics of light, light and vision, the measurement of light, color, and light sources. The application volume discusses approaches to lighting design and the factors to be considered in illuminance selection, including the age of observers. Examines lighting design for various environments, such as the office, industry, residents, and roadways.

LOW VISION AND OPTICAL AIDS

Bailey, I. L.
   1986   The optometric examination of the elderly patient. Pp. 189–209 in A. A. Rosenbloom, Jr., and M. W. Morgan, eds., *Vision and Aging: General and Clinical Perspectives*. New York: Professional Press Books/Fairchild Publications.

Describes special considerations that should be taken in providing vision care to the older patient. Includes a discussion of refraction techniques and visual acuity measurements for both the normally sighted older person and the older patient with low vision. Considers how to prescribe various optical aids to enhance vision for patients with low vision.

Damato, B. E.
   1985   Oculokinetic perimetry: A simple visual field test for use in the community. *British Journal of Ophthalmology* 69:927–931.

A method of visual field examination is described that enables an unsupervised person to carry out self-assessment using only a paper test chart, a record sheet, and a pencil. It is entitled "oculokinetic perimetry" because it is the subject's eye that moves and not the test target. By providing nonophthalmic health care workers with a simple means of performing perimetry in the community, and by allowing susceptible people to carry out self-assessment of the visual fields at home, this test should facilitate the detection and management of glaucoma, especially in underdeveloped countries.

Jose, R. T., ed.
   1983   *Understanding Low Vision*. New York: American Foundation for the Blind.

Written for professionals in the low vision area, covering such topics as low vision assessment and training techniques. The text, although directed at the professional, is sufficiently nontechnical to be appreciated by the lay person. Includes a chapter describing both optical aids for the visually impaired as well as nonoptical forms of assistance. Selected references, including several on optical and nonoptical aids and on geriatric concerns in low vision, are annotated.

Kirchner, C.
   1985   *Data on Blindness and Visual Impairment in the U.S.* New York: American Foundation for the Blind.

Twenty-eight "statistical briefs" originally published in the *Journal of Visual Impairment and Blindness* between 1978 and 1984. The chapters contain data on social, educational, and employment characteristics of visually impaired and blind populations in the United States. Information on service delivery systems is also presented.

GENERAL TEXTS ON VISION AND AGING

Birren, S. E., and Schaie, K. W., eds.
   1985   *Handbook of the Psychology of Aging.* New York: Van Nostrand Reinhold Company.

Comprehensive review and excellent reference source of the literature on the psychological and behavioral aspects of aging. Includes chapters on the theory and methods, biological and social influences on behavior, and applications of psychological knowledge to issues relevant to both the individual and society. Chapters devoted to discussions of behavioral processes cover such topics as vision and aging, speed and behavior, and problem solving.

Rosenbloom, A. A., Jr., and Morgan, M. W., eds.
   1986   *Vision and Aging: General and Clinical Perspectives.* New York: Professional Press Books/Fairchild Publications.

This general text covers a diversity of topics related to vision and aging. Considers vision care for the older adult as part of a broader physiological, psychological, and social context. Several chapters present overviews of normal and pathological ocular changes in the aged. Other chapters address issues related to the delivery of health and vision care to the elderly.

Sekuler, R. S., Kline, D., and Dismukes, K., eds.
   1982   Aging and Human Visual Function. New York: Alan R. Liss, Inc.

A collection of papers based on a symposium sponsored by the Committee on Vision. Many aspects of the effects of age on vision are discussed. Considers, for example, changes in the lens, cataract formation, changes and such visual functions as glare sensitivity, dark adaptation, and visual field loss. Other chapters consider the impacts of aging on visual perception and information processing. Discusses, for example, spatial and temporal vision, attention, and pattern recognition. Methodological issues and the impacts of visual changes on the life of the older person are also explored.

SECURITY CLASSIFICATION OF THIS PAGE *(When Data Entered)*

REPORT DOCUMENTATION PAGE		READ INSTRUCTIONS BEFORE COMPLETING FORM
1. REPORT NUMBER	2. GOVT ACCESSION NO.	3. RECIPIENT'S CATALOG NUMBER
4. TITLE *(and Subtitle)* Work, Aging, and Vision: Report of a Conference		5. TYPE OF REPORT & PERIOD COVERED Technical Report
		6. PERFORMING ORG. REPORT NUMBER
7. AUTHOR(s) Working Group on Aging Workers and Visual Impairment		8. CONTRACT OR GRANT NUMBER(s) N00014-80-C-0159
9. PERFORMING ORGANIZATION NAME AND ADDRESS Committee on Vision National Research Council Washington, D.C.		10. PROGRAM ELEMENT, PROJECT, TASK AREA & WORK UNIT NUMBERS NR 201-124
11. CONTROLLING OFFICE NAME AND ADDRESS Office of Naval Research Arlington, Virginia 22217-5000		12. REPORT DATE February 1987
		13. NUMBER OF PAGES 77
14. MONITORING AGENCY NAME & ADDRESS *(if different from Controlling Office)*		15. SECURITY CLASS. *(of this report)* Unclassified
		15a. DECLASSIFICATION/DOWNGRADING SCHEDULE

16. DISTRIBUTION STATEMENT *(of this Report)*

Approved for Public Release: Distribution Unlimited

17. DISTRIBUTION STATEMENT *(of the abstract entered in Block 20, if different from Report)*

18. SUPPLEMENTARY NOTES

19. KEY WORDS *(Continue on reverse side if necessary and identify by block number)*

Vision
Aging
Visual Function
Committee on Vision
Ophthalmology
Employment

20. ABSTRACT *(Continue on reverse side if necessary and identify by block number)*

The aging of the human eye involves a series of changes in visual performance that can be detected readily in the healthy adult. Viewed in the context of employment, reduced visual function does not necessarily have any effect on job performance, but for some individuals it will. This report reviews what is known about changing visual functions relevant to job performance, and recommends steps that can be taken by the worker and the employer to address changing visual needs.

DD FORM 1473 1 JAN 73 EDITION OF 1 NOV 65 IS OBSOLETE
S/N 0102-LF-014-6601

SECURITY CLASSIFICATION OF THIS PAGE *(When Data Entered)*